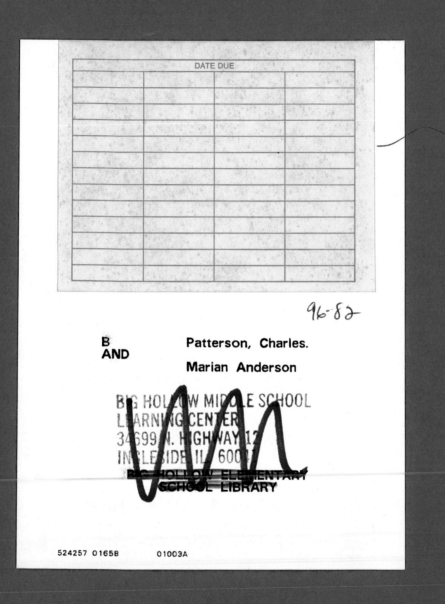

MARIAN ANDERSON

MARIAN ANDERSON

CHARLES PATTERSON

FRANKLIN WATTS
New York / London / Toronto/ /Sydney/ /1988
An Impact Book

Photographs courtesy of:
The Bettmann Archive: p. 91; UPI/Bettmann Newsphotos:
pp. 92, 97, 98, 100, 102, 107; Schomburg Center for
Research in Black Culture, NYPL: pp. 93, 94, 95, 96,
99, 101, 103, 104; AP/Wide World Photos: pp. 105, 106.

Library of Congress Cataloging-in-Publication Data

Patterson, Charles.
Marian Anderson / Charles Patterson.
p.   cm.—(An Impact book)
Bibliography: p.
Includes index.
Summary: A biography of the opera and concert singer who,
among other achievements, was the first black soloist to
perform with the Metropolitan Opera Company in 1955.
ISBN 0-531-10568-7
1. Anderson, Marian, 1902–   . 2. Singers—United States—
Biography. [1. Anderson, Marian, 1902–   . 2. Singers.
3. Afro-Americans—Biography.]   I. Title.
ML420.A6P4   1944
782.1'092'4—dc19
[B]
[92]   88-10695   CIP   AC MN

For Adriane

ACKNOWLEDGMENTS

This is the first book I've written on my computer. I want to give special thanks to my nephew, Bob Patterson, for his help and advice. By setting me up with the right equipment, he delivered me from bondage to my typewriter and led me into the promised land of word processing.

CONTENTS

MARIAN ANDERSON

Growing Up

Born in South Philadelphia, Pennsylvania, on February 17, 1902, Marian Anderson was the first of three daughters born to John and Anna Anderson. Her parents were poor but hardworking, and years later Marian always remembered her childhood with great affection. Her autobiography, *My Lord, What a Morning*, published in 1956, began with these words: "Life with Mother and Father, while he lived, was a thing of great joy."

Marian was only nine years old when her father died, but he left the family with many wonderful memories. Tall and handsome, he towered over Marian's mother. Marian got her height from her father. When she grew up, her mother came up only to her shoulder. John Anderson was a devoted family man who worked very hard. He sold coal and ice, and for many years he worked in the refrigerator room at the Reading Terminal Market.

Marian's mother, Anna, was an educated woman from Lynchburg, Virginia, where she had been a teacher. While her husband was alive, she stayed home and cared for their daughters, but she also took in laundry and did housecleaning to earn extra money for the family.

Early Childhood

After their marriage, John and Anna Anderson rented a room on Webster Street; it was there that Marian was born. When Marian was two and her mother was expecting a new baby, the family moved in with John Anderson's parents, whose house had room for them. Marian's earliest memory was of the room her parents lived in on the third floor of her grandparents' house. Marian crawled under the bed and fell asleep when her mother was about to give birth. When Marian woke up, she heard a cry—the first cry of her new sister, Alyce. Peeking out from under the bed, Marian spotted the doctor's black bag. She was sure that her new baby sister had come out of that black bag.

When the third daughter, Ethel, arrived, the family moved into a rented house on Colorado Street, not far from Marian's grandparents. The house was small, and Anna had to bathe her daughters in a huge wooden tub in the middle of the kitchen floor. Marian sometimes helped her mother after her sisters were put to bed. She cleared the dishes off the dining room table and used her own little carpet sweeper to clean up.

Marian was a happy child. Once when she was sitting by herself in her little chair in the dining room, her mother came in to find out why she was laughing with such delight. To Marian, the flowers on the decorative molding high on the wall looked like the faces of people leaning out of windows and waving at her. The scene looked "like a little town where a lot of people were having a grand time."[1]

While Marian's mother was busy with her housework and with her other chores, Marian and her sisters played with their dolls and with one another. Marian remembered that she spent a lot of time sitting at the table or on a little bench "beating out some sort of rhythm with my hands and feet and la-la-la-ing a vocal accompaniment" that meant nothing to anyone else. Marian wrote that "some people might say that these were the first signs of music in me. I would only say that I felt cozy and happy."

One of the biggest thrills for the Anderson daughters was their annual visit to the Barnum and Bailey Circus. The family always packed a basket for the long trip on the trolley out to the circus grounds. Marian and her sisters were mesmerized by everything that took place under the big tent. At the end of the long day, the family would trudge to the trolley for the ride home.

Christmas and Easter were also happy holidays. Marian's father always bought his daughters new bonnets for Easter. He shopped for them himself to make sure each hat had a bright flower attached. At home, he always took special pleasure in presenting each of his daughters with her new Easter bonnet.

When Marian was very young, she dreamed of becoming a doctor when she grew up. She used to pretend that her doll was ill so that she could nurse it back to health. When one of Marian's friends got hurt, she loved to be the one who put the bandage on.

Early Interest in Music

Marian loved singing at home with her family. Her mother, who grew up singing in church choirs but had no special voice training, had the family sing hymns, spirituals, and old American songs. Marian's father also liked to sing around the house, even though he had no special talent for it.

The Union Baptist Church soon became a very important part of Marian's life, and it was there that she first heard trained choirs. Her father was a special officer at the church. He attended services every Sunday, and he was in charge of the ushers. Marian was still quite young when her father began taking her to church, partly to relieve Anna from the job of always looking after all three girls. Marian attended Sunday school and then sat through the main service, where she got a chance to listen to the singing of the congregation and the senior choir.

Marian was six when she took the step that set her on her course—she joined the junior choir. Because its director, Mr. Robinson, conveyed his love of music to the youngsters and encouraged them to do their best, the junior choir sang with great enthusiasm. They were soon invited to perform for the older children's Sunday school, which met in the afternoon.

Marian's best friend, Viola Johnson, who lived across the street, was also in the choir, so Mr. Robinson arranged to have the two girls sing a duet. He kept playing the melody of the hymn, "Dear to the Heart of the Shepherd," over and over again for them until they remembered it. Then he gave them copies of the music so that they could practice. They rehearsed the hymn many times on their own, with Viola singing the soprano part and Marian the alto. Marian was delighted to have the chance to sing a duet with her best friend. After their performance for the older children, Mr. Robinson was so pleased that he had them sing their duet in front of the congregation at the main Sunday service.

At school, music was Marian's favorite subject. Her classroom was next to the music room, so she got to hear music through the wall. She loved to listen to what the music class was working on, and she sometimes lost track of what her homeroom teacher was saying. When it came time for her class to go to the music room, she already knew the songs.

One day the teacher passed out the music for one of the songs Marian already loved from listening to it through the wall. Marian put back her head and sang it for all she was worth. The puzzled teacher came over and asked her what she was singing. "Sleep, Polly, Sleep," Marian answered. The teacher suggested she look at the music sheet. Marian saw that the words that had sounded like "Sleep, Polly, sleep" were "Peacefully sleep."

Marian was six when she acquired a violin, the first musical instrument she ever owned. When she heard one played in church, she fell in love with it and was determined to have one. She spotted a violin that cost $3.98 hanging in the cluttered window of the pawnshop around the corner from where she lived. Marian scrubbed steps and did errands for pennies and nickels until she had saved enough money to buy the instrument. Then, with the help of an older cousin, she went to the pawnshop and bought the violin.

A friend of the family taught her how to tune it and play a few notes. There was no money available for her to take lessons, so she did the best she could on her own. In the course of Marian's attempt to learn to play, first one string broke and then another. Finally the bridge broke, too. Somebody helped her fix the bridge and replace the strings, but it was no use. The strings kept breaking until finally the violin was a complete wreck. The experience taught Marian that she was not destined to be a violinist.

Marian also wanted to learn ballet and even managed to obtain a pair of ballet slippers. After school, she used to rush home to practice standing on her toes while holding on to the back of a chair. Because she was tall for her age, it did not take long for Marian to decide that she was not the ballet type. She reflected later about her flirtation with ballet, "It is a wonder that I did not tumble on my face and smash my teeth."[2]

When Marian was about eight, she talked her father into buying an old upright piano from his brother. As soon as the movers set the piano in the corner of the Anderson living room, Marian was up on the bench, running her fingers up and down the keyboard. Marian's parents could not afford to pay for lessons, but she managed to get hold of a long white card marked with notes that she set up directly behind the keys. Using the card, Marian could play notes one by one and accompany herself as she sang simple tunes.

One day while Marian was on an errand for her mother, she heard beautiful piano music coming from one of the houses on the street. When she went up the steps and peeked in the window to see where it was coming from, she saw a black woman playing the piano. Marian's mother had always told her, "Remember, wherever you are and whatever you do, someone always sees you." The woman did not know she was being watched by a little girl, who was thinking that if the woman could play the piano like that, she could, too. Years later when Marian did learn to play the piano well enough to accompany herself, she remembered the woman, who had no idea of the effect she was having on a young girl as she played that day.

Marian sang mostly the alto part in the junior choir. She could also have sung soprano, the highest part, if she had been asked, but there were always more sopranos than altos, and she was happy to sing where she was most needed. Mr. Robinson recognized her talent, so he kept giving her more to do. He formed a quartet and had her sing the lowest part. Marian even sang several duets with her father's sister, who was a member of the senior choir. Marian's aunt sang the soprano part, and Marian sang the alto.

Marian's aunt, who was very much interested in the music of other churches, knew a preacher who was starting his own storefront church. She took it upon herself to arrange a fund-raising concert to help him earn money for his new church. When she invited Marian to sing at the concert, Marian agreed, but didn't think anything more about it. Then one day when she was on her way to the grocery store, Marian caught sight of a small handbill lying in the street. She later recalled having a funny feeling about it even before she picked it up. Marian was flabbergasted to see her picture on the handbill. "Come and hear the baby contralto, ten years old," the flyer announced. (Actually, Marian was only eight.) She was so thrilled that when she got home from her errand, she discovered that she had bought potatoes instead of the bread her mother had sent her out to buy.

When Marian's father died, a terrible emptiness filled the house. There had been an accident at work, and he had been struck in the head. He was taken home where he lay helpless in bed over Christmas before finally passing away. His death was a tragic turning point in the life of the family.

Life at Grandmother's

After the funeral, Marian and her family returned to live with her grandparents on Fitzwater Street, where life was very different from before. Marian's aunt managed the house, and Marian's mother did her share of the work, but Marian's grandmother was the real boss, and her word was law. She was a large, imposing woman—tall, stout, and rather formidable. When she wanted somebody, that person came running. Grandmother Anderson spent most of her time during the day sewing, with her basket at her side, but she also played the old-fashioned organ in the parlor. Her body swayed with the steady rhythm of the music as she pressed the pedals with her feet and worked the keys and stops with her hands.

Although Marian's grandfather was much quieter, he, too, was impressive in his own way. Because he was soft-spoken, most people assumed that he was dominated by his wife. However, he was stronger than he seemed, and his wife did not try to push him past a certain point. Marian was intrigued by him because he was a black Hebrew. His Sabbath was on Saturday, which he spent in the temple. Marian first heard the words "unleavened bread" and "Passover" from him, and he deepened her understanding of the spirituals she sang in church.

Marian's new home was much noisier because there were many more children. Besides Marian and her sisters, there were two cousins and two or three other children whom Marian's grandmother looked after while their mothers worked. Grandmother Anderson made sure all the children began their day correctly by eating hot cereal.

When the grandparents' house became too crowded, the entire family moved into a larger house on Christian Street. The living room of this new home was twice as large, so there was more space to spread out. Although the new house was still noisy and crowded, Marian's grandmother kept everybody in order and satisfied. Marian later said the experience of living in her grandmother's house was good for the children because "we learned how to share a room with others, how to understand their ways and respect their rights and privileges."[3]

Marian's mother had to work hard to support her daughters. During the day, she went out to clean houses, and sometimes she brought laundry back as well. However, she never complained about the hard work or about the heat in the summer or about having to wait for a long time on corners for streetcars. She used the money she earned to buy food and cook it for her daughters' supper. Because she did not want her daughters going into their grandmother's or aunt's food supplies, Mrs. Anderson put their food in special containers. She always paid her share of the rent and did her share of the work. Often when she was home on a Sunday or holiday, she cooked for everybody.

Even if Marian had been old enough to work, her mother would not have allowed it. As a former teacher, Anna Anderson believed in education, and she encouraged Marian to take her schooling seriously. However, after Marian completed grammar school, she went on to William Penn High School, where she took the commercial course so that she could learn how to earn money to help her mother and to finance her music studies. For Marian, music was the most important thing in the world, but to pay for her lessons she knew she would have to get a job as soon as possible. A friend of the family said that her husband would give Marian a job if she learned to type and take dictation.

That was good news, but Marian soon discovered that her heart really wasn't in her shorthand and bookkeeping classes. She was happiest in music class, which met only once a week. The music teacher recognized her talent, so Marian sang in the school chorus and did an occasional solo. Once after singing a solo at a school assembly, Marian was summoned to the principal's office. There she heard a visitor who had enjoyed her solo telling the principal, "I don't understand why this girl is taking shorthand and typewriting. She should have a straight college preparatory course and do as much as possible in music."[4]

Senior Choir

Although Marian looked sixteen, she was only thirteen when she was invited to join the senior choir at her church. She did so gladly, although she continued to be a member of the junior choir as well. Singing with both choirs during her teens, Marian felt a deep sense of dedication and responsibility to singing for the church.

Even before Marian had any singing lessons or learned any techniques, her voice showed an amazing strength and versatility. During the services, the senior choir sang from the choir loft at the back of the church where Marian sang out with unfettered youthful exuberance. Sometimes she let herself go so much that gentle suggestions had to be made to get her to recognize that her voice was a little too noticeable.

Even as a teenager, Marian could sing any music that was set in front of her. She was used to singing the alto part, but she could sing the soprano and tenor parts just as effortlessly. Sometimes she even filled in for the baritone or bass, although she usually sang those parts an octave higher. Marian was a choir director's dream. The leader of the senior choir, Mr. Williams, never had to worry about soloists not showing up. Whenever he introduced a new song to the choir, Marian always took the music home and learned all the solo parts. If a soloist did not show up, Marian would step in and sing the part.

Marian became an indispensable member of both choirs, and she never missed a Sunday. The congregation made her feel appreciated and needed, and the minister, the Reverend

Mr. Parks, praised her voice often. The church made Marian feel that she belonged and was a crucial part of what went on there.

The church was important socially as well as musically. Marian joined the youth group—the Baptist Young People's Union—which was composed of boys and girls her age. They were enthusiastic about their activities and very competitive, always trying to outdo one another. Marian entered the speech competition and presented a talk on the Bible. She gave her speech an impressive Latin title. She also entered spelling bees and won several first prizes.

When Marian was transferred to South Philadelphia High School, her new principal, Dr. Lucy Wilson, took a special interest in her. Dr. Wilson believed in interesting assemblies at which students with musical talent were given the chance to perform in front of the student body. Marian sang at several of these school assemblies.

Marian became fascinated by the stage, but she decided that she was not really cut out to be an actress. As a member of the Camp Fire Girls, she was in the chorus line in one of their shows. Although Marian enjoyed being in the show, she had no illusions that she was cut out for the theater. In high school, she occasionally attended performances by a black acting company and was very impressed by the performers. She resolved that if she was ever called on to act, she would like to be as natural and as convincing as they were.

Singing was what mattered most, though, to Marian, and the church became something of a showcase for her talent. Union Baptist was a nationally known black church that people made a point of visiting when they came to Philadelphia. The church liked to do unusual things, especially with its music.

One of the showpieces of the senior choir was "Inflammatus," a song that had a series of high C's for the soprano soloist. One Sunday when the soprano was absent, Mr. Williams motioned to Marian to take her place. As the choir sang "Inflammatus," Marian passed the test magnificently by singing the soprano solo naturally and effortlessly, including all the high C's. Later, after Marian began her formal voice training, she would lose some of that youthful fearlessness and approach those high C's with a certain amount of fear and trepidation. But at the age of thirteen, fourteen, and fifteen, Marian did not worry about what she was doing. She just did it, and somehow it all poured out naturally.

Marian's singing with the senior choir resulted in her first trips to other places. Visitors to the church were often so impressed by the senior choir that they invited the group to sing elsewhere. Sometimes, if the distance was too great or the travel expenses too much for the entire choir, a smaller group—a double quartet, a quartet, a duet, or even a soloist—would represent the church. Marian was frequently chosen to be part of the smaller groups the church sent out, and she was sometimes sent out alone. She made her first trip to New York City as part of a group from the senior choir sent to the Abyssinian Baptist Church, the largest church in Harlem.

Influence of Roland Hayes

The Reverend Mr. Parks loved music and was proud of his church's reputation for musical excellence. Every year, the church presented a gala concert that drew people from all over Philadelphia. Roland Hayes, the accomplished black tenor, was frequently the featured soloist. As one of the foremost interpreters of French songs, German *lieder* (art songs), and spirituals, Hayes was an internationally acclaimed singer. The son of a former slave, he had studied at Fisk University in Nashville and with private teachers in Boston and Europe.

It was from listening to Roland Hayes at these concerts that Marian first heard European music. Hayes sang songs in many languages, and he was renowned for his interpretations of the *lieder* of Schubert and Brahms. Even people who did not know the language of the song or understand music generally knew it was beautiful singing. Black people were proud that the famous Roland Hayes was one of their own. His appearance at the church's annual concert was one of the highlights of the Philadelphia concert season.

Marian was fascinated by Hayes's talent and by the artistry that went into the European songs, but some of the people in the congregation grumbled occasionally that they didn't understand what he was singing. "If our Marian sang," some of them would say to Mr. Parks, "we would understand what *she* was singing about."

Finally, the Reverend Mr. Parks agreed to give them what they wanted. He asked Marian to sing a few selections at the next gala program when Hayes was to perform. Marian was immediately seized by stage fright. Appearing before a large audience did not scare her, but appearing on the same stage with the great Roland Hayes terrified her. How would an internationally recognized concert singer who had sung before kings and queens in Europe feel about appearing with an unknown schoolgirl?

Roland Hayes could not have been nicer or more supportive. When Marian sang at the gala concert, he applauded her songs as heartily as anyone in the audience. When she came back to her seat, he whispered to her that he would like to have a talk with her and her family before he left town. The very next day, he paid a call on the Andersons. He told them that Marian had a great gift and should have instruction to develop her talent. Marian's mother explained that the family did not have money for singing lessons. Also, Marian's grandmother was against voice lessons because, as far as she was concerned, Marian sang just fine the way she did.

The next time Roland Hayes was in Philadelphia, he visited the Andersons again. Once more he urged professional training for Marian in the strongest possible terms and recommended that she study with his own former teacher, Arthur Hubbard, who lived in Boston. He said that he had already spoken to the teacher about Marian and that Mr. Hubbard was willing to take her on as his pupil without charge. Marian could live in his house in return for helping Mrs. Hubbard with some of the housework.

That night, during a family discussion, Marian's grandmother adamantly opposed sending Marian to Boston. She said Marian was too young to live that far away from home. Anyway, she didn't need singing lessons, since she already sang better than any teacher. Marian's mother might have let Marian go to Boston, but Grandmother's word was law. There were more discussions, but Marian's grandmother refused to change her mind.

Help from the Church

One Sunday the Reverend Mr. Parks and the congregation decided to take up a special collection for "our Marian." People gave what they could, and years later Marian remembered the exact amount—$17.02, a good sum of money in those days. The money was turned over to Marian's mother, who was told to use it to buy Marian whatever she needed.

What Marian needed most was a good pair of shoes, but what she most *wanted* was a dress to wear at the next gala concert. Marian's mother took her to Wanamaker's department store where Marian saw exactly what she wanted—a beautiful white silk dress decorated with attractive trim around the neck, sleeves, and hem. However, when they found out the dress cost $14.98, they decided against buying it. Instead, they decided to make Marian a dress, using the collection money to purchase the materials.

Marian and her mother bought some satin, cut it out according to pattern, and put it together using the family sewing machine. Marian trimmed the dress with a braid that was decorated with gold-colored blooms and leaves. This homemade dress was just what Marian wanted and needed, so she wore it proudly at the next gala concert and on many occasions afterward. When people complimented her on her attractive evening dress, she felt good knowing she had helped make it. Since the materials cost $10, she was able to use the rest of the collection money to buy some small things she needed. She had always loved the people of her church, but this collection made her feel even more grateful.

Singing on Her Own

After Marian learned to accompany herself on the piano, she began accepting invitations to sing in other places. When she got home from school, she did her chores and homework, ate quickly, and then rushed off to a singing engagement at the YMCA, the YWCA, or one of the churches. Sometimes she sang at three different places in the same evening. At first she was paid only for her transportation. If she received more, she turned most of it over to her mother.

This singing made Marian more in demand at church, since people who had heard her somewhere else would request a solo. Marian was always glad to sing at church, and her voice never seemed to tire. When the senior choir sang the *Messiah*, Marian sang both the contralto and soprano arias without the slightest problem.

Marian was still in high school when she began singing at larger events and receiving more money. She finally felt confident enough to ask for $5 for every appearance. Each time she was paid $5, she gave a dollar to each of her sisters and $2 to her mother, and she kept the other dollar for herself. She paid for the trolley to and from an engagement until her mother told her that travel expenses should come out of the money she gave her. When Marian began earning more than $5, her mother insisted Marian keep the extra money for herself.

When she was still in high school, Marian joined the Philadelphia Choral Society, a group of black singers who sang for the love of it. This gave her yet another opportunity to do what she loved best. One of the society's officers told Marian's mother, "Mrs. Anderson, I am going to tell you something. You mark my words, one of these days this child is going to earn fifty dollars a night. I say fifty dollars a night. Now, you mark my words." Several years later, when his prophecy came true, the family had a little celebration.

Soon Marian began getting invitations to perform outside of Philadelphia. Roland Hayes often recommended her for programs at black colleges and churches that featured young talent. Sometimes she had to be away for several days at a time. As a result of these trips, Marian missed many classes at high school, but her teachers were understanding. They gave her extra help and allowed her to make up her exams.

First Voice Teacher

Although Marian continued to sing naturally and enthusiastically from the heart, she became convinced that she needed voice training. She was introduced by a family acquaintance, Mr. Butler, to a black music teacher with a wonderful soprano voice. This teacher, Mary Saunders Patterson, had received excellent professional training and had performed a good deal herself. For a dollar a lesson, she agreed to teach Marian everything she knew about singing.

Mr. Butler generously agreed to pay for the lessons out of his own pocket, but Mrs. Patterson told Marian privately that she thought young people should not begin their careers by having obligations to people, no matter how generous and well-meaning they might be. When Marian told her that her family could not afford to pay for the lessons, Mrs. Patterson agreed to teach Marian free of charge.

When Marian started her lessons, she was in her third year of high school. Although she had already been singing in public for several years, she looked blank when Mrs. Patterson asked her how she produced a note. So Mrs. Patterson began by making Marian think about *how* she sang. She taught Marian to throw her voice toward a far corner of the ceiling and to keep it focused on that one spot. At first this was very difficult, but before long Marian learned to project her voice. She soon realized that there were two ways of singing: her old natural way, when she sang without thinking about it, and this new way, which was thoughtful and controlled. For the first time in her life, Marian began thinking about technique.

Giving up old habits was not easy for Marian. Her instinct was always just to sing the way she had always sung, especially when she was presented with a new song, but under Mrs. Patterson's watchful eye, she learned to pace herself and to think of her voice as something to be conserved and strengthened by exercise. "Think of your voice as capital you put in a bank," Mrs. Patterson told her. "You want to draw on the interest, not deplete the capital."

Mrs. Patterson also introduced Marian to her first Schubert song, "Die Rose, die Taube, die Lillie."

Rejection

Mrs. Patterson encouraged Marian to think about attending music school. "If you are serious about your music and want to go on with it," she said, "you really ought to learn more than I can teach you." Marian talked it over with her mother, and they agreed that the idea of attending a music school in the Philadelphia area was worth looking into. Certainly the family could not afford to pay a high fee, but maybe scholarships were available. They agreed that their first step was to get the information.

Early one morning at registration time, Marian went by trolley to a music school in Philadelphia. She felt excited when she saw the window marked Registrar. Marian got in the long line and waited patiently. When she finally reached the window, the young white girl scowled and looked right past her to the next person in line. Marian was so surprised by the young woman's rudeness that she stood to one side to try to understand what was happening. One person after another went to the window to ask questions and request forms. This went on until there were no people left in line except Marian. The girl then turned to Marian. "What do *you* want?"

Her voice felt like a knife cutting into Marian. The girl was Marian's age, someone Marian might have gone to school with, but when Marian asked for a registration form, the girl looked at her coldly. "We don't take colored," she said. Then she slammed down the window.

Marian was stunned and humiliated, but she didn't say a word. She was shocked that someone so young could say such a thing, and she could not believe what she heard coming from such a well-respected music school. Marian was deeply hurt, but it was not in her character to argue or demand to see the girl's superior. Marian knew about prejudice because she had heard people talking about it, but this was her first personal contact with the brutal reality of racism. It was as if a cold bucket of water had suddenly been poured on her hopes and dreams. Shaken, she turned and walked out of the school.

Marian talked to her mother about what had happened, just as she talked to her mother about everything. She did not discuss the incident with others. Her mother encouraged her to keep her faith and not give up on her dreams. If Marian was meant to be a professional singer, God would find a way. If Marian's aunt had found out about this experience, she would have raised a protest and demanded to know the official policy of the school, but Marian and her mother were similar in the quieter way they reacted to things. "That music school no longer exists in Philadelphia, and its name does not matter," Marian reflected years later. But she still felt hurt by the rejection, saying, "True enough, my skin was different, but not my feelings."[5]

Although Marian grew up in an integrated neighborhood where for the most part blacks and whites lived together without incident, she and her sisters heard relatives and family friends talk about race problems. Marian knew about stores where blacks were not welcome or had to wait longer for service. She also knew that trolleys sometimes passed by black people waiting on the corner. There had always been some white girls Marian could play with and some she couldn't, just as there were some parties Marian and her sisters went to and others they didn't. But they had learned to accept this. They didn't want to go to places where they weren't welcome or associate with people who didn't want to be with them.

After her rejection, Marian dropped the idea of going to music school. She wondered what the attitude of other schools might be and did not want to risk another rejection. Her mother helped her keep the incident in perspective and encouraged her to have faith that a way would be found. Marian's mother was much less aggressive than her aunt, but she had her own strong sense of right and wrong, and she taught Marian to believe that a way could always be found to overcome any obstacle.

Marian's first experience with segregation in the South came when she traveled with her mother to Savannah, Georgia, where Marian had a singing engagement. In Washington, they changed trains and were sent to a segregated car set aside for blacks. Marian was shocked. The car was dark and stuffy, and the windows were so dirty that it was hard to see out of them. If the windows were opened for air, the soot and smoke from the train's engine filled the car.

On trains in the South, blacks were excluded from the dining car and sleeping berths, which were reserved for whites only. Blacks had to bring their own food or buy it from a vendor on the train. At every stop, there were separate waiting rooms for whites and blacks. Now Marian saw for herself just how poor the black waiting rooms were and how humiliating it was for those who had to use them.

When Marian returned from Savannah, she was "a bit wiser but sadder and so ashamed." Years later Marian remembered this first exposure to segregation: "I had looked closely at my people on that train. Some seemed to be embarrassed to the core. Others appeared to accept the situation as if it were beyond repair. Habit, I thought, can be good if it has an elevated aim; it can be devastating if it means taking bad things for granted; and I wondered how long it would take people on both sides to seek a change."[6]

Despite Marian's experience with segregation and racial prejudice, she always remained an optimist, but a realistic one. In her autobiography, written before the civil rights movement of the 1960s began, Marian said, "Things are changing in our country, and I am hopeful." Then she added, "But I cannot suppress a private regret. I still wish that I could have gone to music school."[7]

CHAPTER 2

Early Career

Mrs. Patterson urged Marian to continue her voice lessons with a teacher who could offer her more advanced training, so Marian's next music teacher was Agnes Reifsnyder, who had a good reputation in Philadelphia. Agnes Reifsnyder, a contralto, worked more on Marian's medium and lower tones, a range that Marian found more comfortable. In the two years she worked with Marian, she taught her to concentrate on her breathing and gave her more exercises to help her focus her singing. She also introduced Marian to the songs of Brahms and other European composers and worked with her to develop entire programs for the concerts Marian was giving out of town.

Giuseppe Boghetti

Shortly before Marian graduated from high school, Dr. Lucy Wilson, the principal who had taken such an interest in her singing, arranged for Marian to meet Giuseppe Boghetti, a well-known voice teacher who had trained many famous concert singers and opera stars. Getting an appointment with the master was no easy accomplishment, but Lisa Roma, Dr. Wilson's friend, who had heard Marian sing at one of the high school assemblies, was one of Mr. Boghetti's students. She made the arrangements for Marian to meet him.

Dr. Wilson and Lisa Roma accompanied Marian to Mr. Boghetti's studio. When they arrived, Mr. Boghetti announced that he already had more students than he could handle. A short man with unruly black hair, he could be gruff and impatient. He made it clear that he would listen to Marian sing only as a favor to Miss Roma. Dr. Wilson was taken aback by his abruptness, and so was Marian.

When Marian handed him the music to the spiritual she chose to sing—"Deep River"—Mr. Boghetti said he had never heard of it. However, he sat down at this piano and played the introduction. Marian then closed her eyes and sang from her heart the great spiritual about "that promised land" over the Jordan River. After she finished, there was a long silence. Marian just waited, not looking at Mr. Boghetti. Finally Mr. Boghetti broke the silence by asking her to sing a scale.

When she finished, Mr. Boghetti said, "I will make room for you right away, and I will need only two years with you. After that, you will be able to go anywhere and sing for anybody." Marian felt elated, but the mood faded quickly as Mr. Boghetti started talking about his fees, assuming the lessons would begin right away. Marian's heart sank as she realized that she could not afford lessons at those prices. She was earning more money from singing than she ever had, and her mother was now working as a department store cleaning woman, but Marian wanted her mother to stop working. She looked so worn and thin that Marian worried about her. Also, Marian's sisters had more expenses than ever, now that they were in high school—shoes, books, gym clothes. Marian told Mr. Boghetti she could not afford the lessons.

On the way back from the studio, Dr. Wilson told Marian not to feel discouraged. A way would be found, she said, and Dr. Wilson was right. Once more Marian's neighbors and friends at the church came to the rescue. They arranged a gala concert at the church, with Roland Hayes as one of the soloists. They raised $600 for Marian's singing lessons, and her studies with Giuseppe Boghetti began immediately.

Marian soon learned why Mr. Boghetti had asked her to sing the scale. Although he was very impressed by Marian's natural talent, he discovered an uneven tone quality in several places in her singing. He set out to correct this problem immediately. He had Marian hum notes until she felt their vibration and then had her place the note exactly where she had been humming.

Marian soon realized that she was still fighting against changing her old spontaneous way of singing into a consistently disciplined one, even though she had already studied with two teachers. Mr. Boghetti's method of having her focus her voice inside her head proved to be more practical than Mrs. Patterson's approach. In a concert hall, it was not always easy for her to find the right corner to use as a target, so focusing the music internally gave Marian a method that she could use in any physical setting.

Giuseppe Boghetti found out that Marian's best tone was E flat, so he used that note as the starting point and the model for all the other tones. Then he built exercises that moved up and down from it. In this way, he was able to help Marian develop an even, unbroken vocal line up and down her singing range from her lowest to her highest tone.

Mr. Boghetti gave Marian exercises to help with an aspect of her singing she had never worked on—her breathing. He had her hold her hands against her ribs, and by breathing slowly, see how much she could expand her rib cage. This constant expansion of Marian's abdominal muscles strengthened Marian's breathing and gave her greater vocal power.

He also worked on the full range of Marian's voice. With the help of the exercises he gave her, she moved up to an A, to a B, and then finally to a high C. The B and C provided extra insurance for the A that Marian used frequently in her concert singing. Doing the exercises rapidly and lightly also helped improve Marian's vocal agility.

Other people used to tell Marian that since she could hit high C without any difficulty, she should sing Aïda. But Marian resisted the idea. "The fact that you can emit a screech on high C," she said, "does not give you the right to sing

Aïda, not by a long shot. I knew perfectly well that I was a contralto, not a soprano. Why Aïda?"[1]

Sometimes Marian sang scenes from the opera *Aïda* with Mr. Boghetti just for the fun of it. Earlier in his career as a tenor, he had dreamed of singing opera, so he loved to have Marian join him occasionally in singing the scene between Radames and Amneris from Act IV. Marian enjoyed the singing as much as Mr. Boghetti did, but it would be many years before she finally sang in an opera.

With Mr. Boghetti as her teacher, Marian learned many of the songs that later became part of her repertory—Schubert, Brahms, Schumann, and Hugo Wolf in German; Italian arias; songs in French; Rachmaninoff and other Russians in English translation; and songs by American and English composers. Mr. Boghetti always looked for places where the word did not fit the tone exactly and then concentrated on that passage by creating special exercises to solve the problem.

Under his direction, Marian developed a completely professional attitude toward her singing. She regarded the exercises as important tools for achieving the ability to perform her best under all circumstances. "There is no shortcut," she said later. "You must understand the how and why of what you are doing. If you do, you can give an acceptable performance even if you are indisposed. You cannot say, 'Tonight I don't feel good and I won't appear.' You have to be prepared to carry on even on nights when you would rather do anything else but perform."[2]

Even though Marian's concert schedule increased in the years ahead and she often had to be away for long periods in Europe, she always came back to Mr. Boghetti, who went over her programs with her and helped her correct every error. Marian knew that under the pressure of a busy schedule, it was all too easy to slip back into old habits; she was grateful to Mr. Boghetti for catching any lapses that escaped her attention.

Mr. Boghetti had no patience with students who did not

practice, and he accepted no excuses. But Marian had enormous demands on her time. Because she did so much public singing, both in Philadelphia and out of town, she had to work extra hard to do all her homework.

Marian often had to cram her preparation for Mr. Boghetti into the days just before her lesson. The night before her voice lesson, she would take her music to bed with her and study the notes for as long as she could stay awake. Then at school the next day, she would steal glances at the music whenever she could. By the time she reached the studio, she was so immersed in her lesson that Mr. Boghetti would be impressed by how well she had prepared that week.

For those less dedicated than Marian, Mr. Boghetti could be a terrifying teacher. He made no bones about his lack of respect for dilettantes, and he often said that he would not teach "society people who think it would be nice to sing." He respected the seriousness of Marian's commitment and sometimes let her stay on after her lesson was over so that she could listen to more advanced pupils.

Because Marian treasured her training sessions so much, she was always conscious that she had only thirty minutes for her lesson and that there was always somebody else waiting for his turn. Sometimes when Mr. Boghetti interrupted the lesson to explain something, Marian would think of the precious minutes slipping away. When she talked, she had the feeling that Mr. Boghetti was watching the clock just as anxiously. At times when the next pupil was late or did not show up, Mr. Boghetti let Marian stay on beyond her allotted time, an unexpected gift of extra minutes for which Marian was always grateful.

Mr. Boghetti respected Marian's talent and hard work so much that when the lesson money her friends and neighbors had raised ran out, he looked for ways to keep the lessons going. One of his friends wanted to advance $250 for Marian's lessons in return for her promise to appear in some concerts for him, but neither Mr. Boghetti nor Marian felt right about an offer that was so vague. For more than a year, Mr. Boghetti continued to teach Marian without getting paid; at one point, he even offered to cancel her debt. However, Marian would not hear of it. She was determined to pay him in full. Eventually she began to earn more money for her concerts, and she even earned extra money by giving singing lessons of her own. In this way, she was finally able to repay her debt.

Marian loved to attend concerts, but she did not have the money to attend as many as she would have liked. Nonetheless, she did manage to hear the accomplished contralto, Ernestine Schumann–Heink, and the mezzo-soprano, Sigrid Onegin, when they came to Philadelphia. Hearing the expert way these great singers sang foreign languages, especially German, inspired Marian and made her aware of just how much she had to learn.

Marian knew she had to learn European languages, but she did not have the money, the time, or the opportunity to study them formally. She studied French in high school, and Mr. Boghetti helped her with her Italian pronunciation. However, Marian did not know any German. The best she could do with *lieder* was to memorize the words and then sing them without really knowing what they meant.

Marian's language problem was once pointed out to her in an especially embarrassing way. After a program at the University of Pennsylvania, where she sang for forty-five minutes, a young instructor of foreign languages, who was very impressed with Marian's voice, was so concerned about her pronunciation that he took the trouble to find out where she lived and to pay her a visit. He told Marian and her mother with great earnestness that a person with such a beautiful voice had no business singing foreign languages so badly. Marian knew the young man was right. It was a truth that would be driven home even more painfully later.

This experience only strengthened an idea that had been growing in Marian for some time, although she was in no position to do anything about it yet. She knew deep down that she had to study in Europe someday, as Roland Hayes had done. Lawrence Brown, who was Roland Hayes's accompanist, had been the first to suggest to Marian that she think about studying abroad, and he had even recommended Raimund von Zur Mühlen, who lived in England, as the best teacher for her. Not only was he respected internationally, but he was one of the world's greatest interpreters of German *lieder*. Studying with Mr. Boghetti, who had been trained in Europe and whose musical style Marian found so appealing, only strengthened her secret desire to study in Europe.

Marian later admitted that she might not have practiced as much as she should have, but not because she did not want to. The problem was that she was a sensitive young woman who was unwilling to disturb other people with her voice training. A more aggressive person might not have cared as much, but Marian was not that kind of person. At home, there were other people to think about, and Marian would not sing when she thought it would disturb them. She tried to make up for it by singing softly or even singing internally in a sort of musical whisper.

When Marian sang in Chicago at a convention for black musicians, they were so impressed that they voted to help finance her musical education. Some of the people at the convention even pledged money, and it was agreed that Marian should apply to the Yale School of Music. Marian did apply and was accepted, but she never enrolled because not enough money materialized to pay the tuition.

King Fisher

Marian grew up being friends with boys, but she did not have boyfriends as such. One little boy was her good friend when she was small, but after that her close friends were girls. As a teenager, Marian did have crushes on boys and did her share of pining away over them. Sometimes she wrote down the names of boys she knew and then mooned over the one she liked best.

However, for Marian, there was to be one special young man. His full name was Orpheus H. Fisher, but everybody called him King. They met in Wilmington, Delaware, while they were both still in school. Marian had gone to Wilmington to appear at a benefit concert, and afterward there was a reception at the home of a Mr. Fisher. As Marian went up the steps to the front door of the house, her way was blocked by a young light-skinned black man in a playful mood. At first, Marian was amused, but when the young man persisted in keeping her from entering the house, she grew annoyed. When she finally got inside, she met another young man, who looked just like the one on the porch but was a bit shorter. Marian didn't pay much attention to either of them, since she really only wanted to say hello to the host and some of the guests before taking the train back to Philadelphia.

Several weeks later, the doorbell rang at home, and Marian's sister came to tell her that a Mr. Fisher was there to see her. Marian had forgotten about the Wilmington incident. She told her sister to tell the person she didn't know anybody by that name. Soon her sister returned and told Marian that the visitor knew her because she was in his house in Wilmington. The visitor was King's older brother, the shorter of the two young men. He stayed for a while and then left. He said he would come back, and he did—the same day!

The young man visited Marian often, but then one day he arrived with his younger but taller brother, the one who had teased Marian in Wilmington by blocking her way at the front door of his house. After that, the Fisher brothers came together often to Marian's house.

One day while they were sitting and talking in Marian's living room, King put his arm across the back of the couch and touched Marian's shoulder. When she looked at him, he slipped her a folded note without his brother noticing. After they left, she read the note, which said, "This affair between you and my brother has got to stop."

Marian thought that was ridiculous. She was not having an affair. But it was the first time King showed he was interested in Marian, and before long he, not his older brother, became Marian's boyfriend. Since King was studying in Philadelphia, he spent as much time as he could at Marian's house.

Eventually, matters became serious enough between them that King took Marian home to Wilmington to meet his family. First, they went to the homes of King's three older married sisters, and then they had dinner with his parents and brothers. Marian knew that King was thinking about marriage, even though he never talked about it directly. Since she was in the early stages of her singing career, marriage was not something *she* was thinking about.

Once King actually suggested that they elope, but Marian told him not to be silly. Another time when they were visiting Wilmington, King stopped in front of the home of somebody he knew and suggested they look at the house. Marian followed him up the steps to the front door. When she asked him why he wanted to see the house, King answered, "I'm going to see if she has a little apartment where we can live." On hearing that, Marian beat a hasty retreat down the steps.

Although their careers—her singing, his architecture—caused them to go separate ways for many years, they did keep in touch, and somehow they knew that if and when it came time for them to marry, they would marry each other.

Billy King

Mrs. Patterson had been the first person to suggest that Marian think about having her own accompanist. The idea of teaming up with a pianist excited Marian because she was sure that having a good accompanist would improve her singing. That way she could concentrate totally on her singing without having to worry about accompanying herself on the piano or using a strange accompanist supplied for the occasion.

Mrs. Patterson recommended a talented young musician, Billy King, but Marian could not imagine he would be interested. Billy was the organist and choirmaster of a local Episcopal church, and he had served as the accompanist for many guest artists who came to Philadelphia. He had even accompanied Roland Hayes several times. He was a popular and gifted musician, whom many people thought had the potential to be truly outstanding if he applied himself. His parents had always hoped he would be more ambitious. Once his mother told him in front of Marian, "Be careful, Billy. Don't let Marian pass you. She may come up to you and pass you."

Billy King was accompanying Lydia McClain, a beautiful Philadelphia soprano, when Mrs. Patterson recommended him, but Marian could not imagine competing with Lydia. However, one night at the YWCA, when Marian was sitting down at the piano, she suddenly found Billy King next to her, asking her in a whisper if she would let him play for her. Marian was so excited that she barely got through the first song, but she knew that with Billy King at the piano, her singing never sounded better. Although Billy did not become Marian's regular accompanist right away, he did play for her when she and Lydia sang on the same program.

That winter when Lydia and Marian were asked to sing at a church in Orange, New Jersey, four of them took the train—Lydia, Marian, Billy, and a handsome doctor, a friend of Lydia's, who came along just to hear Lydia sing, or so Marian and Billy thought. When the four of them reached the station in Orange, Lydia and her friend announced that they were staying on the train. Marian was puzzled, but she felt better when Billy assured her that Lydia would show up at the church on time. The concert wasn't for several hours, and they probably just wanted some time to themselves before the performance.

However, when it came time for the concert, Lydia was nowhere to be seen. When the woman in charge of the program demanded to know where Lydia was, Marian and Billy told her she would be along any moment. When Lydia didn't show up, Marian went in front of the small audience and sang the entire program herself. Lydia never did show up, and later Marian and Billy found out why—she and her doctor friend had gone to New York and gotten married!

As Marian and Billy waited around after the concert to be paid, they got the impression that everybody was avoiding them. Marian's fee was supposed to be $25, and out of that she had to pay Billy and pay for their round-trip train tickets. Finally, when one of the women asked them solemnly to come with her to the pastor's study, Marian and Billy knew something was wrong.

There were several women in the study. The one in charge of the program said to Marian, "You saw for yourself that we didn't have many people in the audience tonight, and we want to know what you are going to do about it."

Although Marian felt on the spot, she tried to be reasonable. She even offered to contribute part of the six dollars it had cost to rent the piano. "Is that the best you can do?" the woman asked. The rest of the women sat in glum silence, obviously waiting for Marian to waive the fee. Marian felt mortified, but she did not give in. Finally, the woman told the treasurer to give Marian the money they owed her.

At this time, Marian took on a manager, a man by the name of G. Grant Williams, who was the editor of a black Philadelphia newspaper. He had told Marian's grandmother he could help Marian by getting her concerts in other cities through his contacts with other black newspapers. With the blessing of her grandmother, he began arranging Marian's concerts, but he soon became ill, and Billy King had to take over his duties. Billy remained Marian's pianist, but now he also took on the job of preparing the pamphlets and fliers that advertised Marian's singing engagements.

Marian's second experience with segregation came when she and Billy traveled by train to a concert in the South. Billy asked the porter about the chances of getting some hot food from the dining car. The porter went to the dining car and came back to tell Billy and Marian that if they appeared at a certain time they could get some food.

As they passed through the car reserved for whites, Marian noticed how much cleaner and nicer their coach was. Even though the dining car was empty, they had to be seated at the end where the waiters ate and where there was a curtain just in case a waiter was still finishing his meal when whites arrived. Marian and Billy got a hot meal and were treated well. The chef and waiters went out of their way to make them feel comfortable and gave them extra-large portions of food as their way of saying they were glad the two young people had the courage to come to the dining car.

As she sang more and more concerts in the South, Marian knew she had to get used to segregated travel. She needed to arrive at her destination rested and relaxed for her performance, but that was often not possible. Usually she had to try to sleep in her seat on the train. If she was lucky enough to book a vacant berth, other problems arose. When she used the washroom in the morning, she could never be sure of the reaction she would get. One woman might say a friendly good morning, while another might give her a dirty look or mutter something under her breath. Traveling under these conditions created its own special kind of tension, but Marian tried not to let it upset her.

Once on a trip to Hampton, Virginia, when she was traveling by herself, segregation was temporarily suspended because of a storm. In Washington, all the trains heading south were delayed because of a washout, so the passengers had to spend the night in the station. In the morning when a train was finally ready, no effort was made to separate the races because of the unexpected emergency. As black and white passengers sat together, Marian saw a white woman hold a black woman's baby so that the mother could get some sleep. Blacks and whites talked to one another and shared newspapers and even food. Recalling the event later, Marian observed, "The world did not crumble."

After Marian graduated from high school, she and Billy were able to go on longer tours, and, without schoolwork, Marian was able to sing more concerts and prepare for them much more extensively. When they began practicing in a secluded room at Billy's home, Marian did not have to worry so much about disturbing people.

Progress

Billy's contacts helped Marian enormously. He had accompanied singers in many different towns and cities, and he was on good terms with the singers and music lovers who came to his church. Marian began touring more than she ever had, and her earnings increased. Not only did her fee reach the $50 mark that the family friend had once predicted for her, but with Billy as her manager, her fee soon reached $100.

That was not all profit, of course. Billy's share and all the travel expenses—primarily train fare and food—had to come out of the fee. Usually, they did not have hotel expenses. When they traveled to colleges, Marian sometimes stayed in a visitor's room and Billy in the men's dormitory. When they performed at a church, Marian often stayed with one of the women of the church and Billy at the local Y or at another private home. Still, there was not much left once the expenses were subtracted from the fee. However, because Marian had many more concert dates, she was earning more money than she ever had in her life. Best of all, she was earning it by doing what she most loved.

Marian and her mother and sisters had lived with her grandmother, aunt, and cousins for many years, but when a small house was put up for sale by an Irish family right across from her grandmother's on South Martin Street, they decided to buy it. Marian's mother had been left some money by her father, and Marian had saved her concert earnings, so that between the two of them they were able to put up enough money to purchase their first home since Marian's father died.

The signing of the deed was an occasion of great joy. After the occupants of the house moved out, Marian and her family had hardwood floors put in and bought furniture on the installment plan. When the family finally moved in, they invited all their neighbors and friends in to see their "dream house." Marian even set up a studio for herself on the second floor, although because the house was close to other houses, Marian never completely got over her feeling that she might be disturbing others. But at least she now had a place at home to sing and practice.

Marian's increased earnings also allowed the family to purchase certain things they had always wanted. For a long time, they had used a portable phonograph loaned to them by a friend. Even the records Marian loved to play were borrowed. Her favorite recording was *The Barber of Seville*, whose coloratura runs and trills she sang right along with Galli-Curci. When she returned the phonograph and records, she felt a little guilty knowing how many times she had played them. The family eventually bought a large radio-phonograph that remained their pride and joy for many years.

Marian used to visit the home of Dr. Hirsch, who played in an amateur orchestra and liked to invite musicians to his house to perform. One evening Marian sang one of her favorite spirituals, "Heaven, Heaven." At the insistence of the guests, she sang it four times! One of the most enthusiastic listeners, who turned out to be in the record business, asked Marian if she could sing the song the same way in a record studio. When Marian said she thought she could, the man arranged a date for her to go to the Victor recording plant in Camden, New Jersey. Mr. Boghetti helped Marian prepare

"Heaven, Heaven" and "Deep River" and then went with her to the studio where Marian made her first recording.

Marian did not hear the record after it was made and promptly forgot about it in all the excitement of buying furniture for the new house. One day many weeks later, when Marian was in a store with her sister, she heard a phonograph playing "Deep River." When the salesman saw that Marian was looking puzzled, he asked her if she recognized the voice. She said she didn't, but then her sister exclaimed, "It's Marian!"

Marian was stunned. When it dawned on her that it really was her voice, she felt her heart pounding so much that she wanted to run out of the store. Later, when Marian received a copy of the record, she could not listen to it when other people were around. "I could not bear to hear my voice coming out of the machine even when Mother and my sisters were about," she said. "I can't explain why."[3]

As Marian sang in churches, schools, clubs, and halls in many cities and towns, her reputation grew. Whenever a local promoter booked her into a real theater, Marian felt especially good, because the best-known performers appeared in theaters. She also felt good when she learned that her singing was beginning to attract the attention of serious music lovers. When she was finally invited to sing at the Philadelphia Academy of Music, she knew that her singing career had reached a new level.

These were years of personal as well as musical growth for Marian. Because Marian and Billy traveled extensively, mostly in the South, Marian got to see many different places and meet hundreds of people. She performed at all kinds of black schools and colleges—everywhere from the Hampton Institute in Virginia and Howard University in Washington to one-room schoolhouses in backwoods areas. Although she never got over the discomfort of traveling on segregated trains, she met many wonderful people on her tours.

A black couple by the name of Lee made an especially

strong impression on Marian. They lived in rural Virginia where Mr. Lee was the head of a school that pioneered in educating poor children. Marian and Billy were both moved by the dedication of the Lees. When they performed at the Lees' school, they asked only a minimum fee, and sometimes only expense money. Marian suspected that even that amount came out of the Lees' own pockets rather than out of the school budget. The piano was in bad shape, but Marian and Billy loved the Lees and their children so much that they kept coming back.

Marian was impressed and moved by people who did good work quietly and without fanfare, people like the Lees who gave their heart and soul to the children in their school. "There must be modest institutions like that all over the South, built on the determination and love of one or two persons," she said later. "I wonder how many Negro children owe their basic education and perspectives to people like the Lees."[4]

Another personal highlight for Marian was her regular visit to the Hampton Institute, one of the most prestigious black institutions of higher learning in the country. There she befriended Robert Nathaniel Dett, the director of the Hampton Choir and himself a highly respected composer and pianist. A graduate of Oberlin College and the Eastman School of Music, Mr. Dett had studied in Paris with Nadia Boulanger and had written many choral and piano pieces. He had made the Hampton Choir into one of the very best in the world. Many of the students he inspired went on to musical careers of their own.

Mr. Dett took a personal interest in Marian's career and advised her carefully and wisely. His own excellent musical education and experience in Europe inspired Marian to be the best singer she could, and his personal integrity strengthened her own thoughts about music and life. Whenever Marian sang with the Hampton Choir, she knew the choir would perform at the highest level. Mr. Dett took pains to obtain

Marian's program well in advance in order to prepare her songs; the choir always sang the music with the greatest understanding and feeling.

Mr. Dett gave Marian a piece of advice she never forgot. He told her never to compromise when it came to her singing or to the hard work she would have to put in to reach her goals. Even if she never achieved all her goals, he said, the effort to make her dreams come true would be worth all the sacrifice.

The more Marian continued her heavy schedule of concerts and her training with Mr. Boghetti, the more she felt her voice growing in range and maturity. In 1923, she won a singing contest in Philadelphia sponsored by the Philharmonic Society. When local newspapers reported that the winner was a twenty-one-year-old black woman—the first black ever to win the contest—more white people took notice of Marian's singing. That pleased Marian, because she wanted to sing for the widest possible audience.

Marian felt her strength as a singer in a special way for the first time at a performance in Washington, sponsored by Howard University, before an audience of both whites and blacks. She had chosen a group of songs by Richard Strauss, including a piece called "Morgen." Although this song had not seemed too difficult when she began preparing for the concert, she found out as the concert drew closer that there was more to the piece than she had thought. She also realized that by singing "Morgen," she was reaching for a higher level of accomplishment.

When Marian sang "Morgen" at the concert that afternoon, she felt a strength and confidence in her ability she had never known before. She saw the looks of wonder and the smiles of appreciation on the black and white faces in the audience and realized the powerful effect her singing was having. It was a moment that made all the years of struggle seem worthwhile. Marian knew she was experiencing that special mix of exaltation and completeness an artist feels who is at one with her art. As a result of that concert, Marian was sure she could reach any goal she set for herself. She felt a new surge of ambition. She now knew that if she ever failed to achieve a goal she set for herself, she could only blame herself for not applying enough concentration and effort.

Town Hall Disaster

With this new sense of confidence, larger fees, bigger audiences, and favorable reviews, Marian was determined to reach that next higher level of achievement. She felt that she was now ready for the next big challenge. Unfortunately, it was a plunge that nearly ended her career.

New York was the music capital of the country. Any American singer who wanted to make it had to make it there sooner or later. Marian had sung in Harlem, but she had never appeared downtown. Once after a sellout performance in Harlem, the young promoter who managed the concert assured Marian that he could arrange a downtown engagement, and Marian agreed to let him try. When he told her he was going to engage the prestigious Town Hall in the heart of Manhattan, Marian was excited at the prospect of making it big in New York. A successful concert in Town Hall with good reviews by the New York critics would put her on the musical map. She would then be invited to perform in the finest concert halls in America. At age twenty-two, Marian would be on her way to national stardom.

However, she was taking a big risk, since the business arrangements for a New York concert were unlike those of other concerts. She would have to put up the money for the hall and all the other expenses with no guarantee that enough tickets could be sold to cover the costs. She would not receive a set fee, as she normally did. A white singer in this situation usually had a wealthy patron of the arts to sponsor him or her and put up the money for the debut. Because Marian had no such patron, she would have to take the financial risk herself. When the young promoter informed her he had, in fact, reserved Town Hall, Marian committed herself to the concert.

In planning her program, Marian decided not to sing only spirituals, since she did not want to be judged as a black singer, but rather as a singer who happened to be black. With Mr. Boghetti's help, she spent several months preparing her program. It included Brahms's "Von ewiger Liebe" and three other songs she had never sung before. She worked very hard on the pronunciation of the French, Italian, and German songs she had chosen for her program. Because she had never studied German, with its difficult guttural sounds, Marian had to learn the words of the *lieder* painstakingly sound by sound and then practice them over and over again.

On the day of the concert—April 23, 1924—Marian followed precisely the schedule that Mr. Boghetti had advised. She took a morning train from Philadelphia to New York and then a cab to the Y in Harlem. It would have been better for Marian to stay closer to Town Hall, but blacks were not welcome in midtown hotels at that time. At four o'clock, Marian ate supper and rested. Then she prepared and went to Town Hall, arriving at seven o'clock, an hour and a half before the concert. Mr. Boghetti had said that she would then have enough time to go through her voice exercises without feeling rushed. At eight, Billy King joined her backstage in the artist's room, and for the next half-hour, they watched the clock expectantly.

Marian had been told that the tickets, which had been on sale for a long time, were selling well. When Marian had asked earlier how things were going out in the hall, she was assured that a good-size audience was expected. When eight-thirty arrived, Marian and Billy waited for the signal to go out on stage and begin, but nobody came back to notify them. As it got later and later, Marian began to worry. Finally, at nine o'clock, a half-hour after the concert was scheduled to begin, the young promoter came back and, with a little shrug, told them they might as well begin.

When Marian walked onto the stage and looked out at the hall, her heart sank. There was a scattering of people up front and a few farther back, but the rest of the great hall was empty. Now Marian realized that the concert had been delayed in the vain hope that more people would show up. She felt devastated. The excitement and enthusiasm that had been building up in her for months seemed to drain out of her all at once.

Marian bowed to the sparse audience and forced a smile. Her first number—Handel's "Ombra mai fu"—required organ accompaniment, so Billy was far away at the organ at the side of the stage. That left Marian feeling abandoned and miserably alone in the middle of the stage. She had thought she was ready for anything, but she had never expected this.

Marian sang her program as best she could, but the Brahms songs, especially "Von ewiger Liebe," proved especially difficult. The sparse audience applauded after every song, but the sound of their scattered clapping only seemed to draw more attention to the emptiness of the vast hall. The program seemed to drag on forever, but finally Marian made it to the end. She did not feel good about her performance, especially the Brahms songs. What reviews there were in the newspapers the next day only confirmed her feeling. One critic said, "Marian Anderson sang her Brahms as if by rote."

Marian was completely demolished. She had reached for the stars and had fallen flat on her face. Crushed and miserable, she returned to Philadelphia, certain she had let everybody down—her family, Mr. Boghetti, Mr. Dett, Billy, and all the people at the church who had supported her over the years. She blamed herself for making her debut in one of the world's greatest concert halls before she was ready. Feeling discouraged and defeated, she was sure that she never wanted to sing another note and that her musical career was over.

For weeks, even months, after her Town Hall disaster, Marian retreated into herself. She even stopped going to Mr. Boghetti's studio, because her heart wasn't in it. Mr. Boghetti understood her disappointment, so he did not make an issue of it. He was confident that when her wounds healed, Marian would be back. As usual, Marian's mother was a source of comfort and understanding. Her patience and support helped Marian get through this difficult period.

Marian did not blame the critics for their harsh reviews, because she knew they were right. She had been wrong to put herself in such a position. When she said she wanted her singing to please everybody, her mother told her, "Whatever you do in this world, no matter how good it is, you will never be able to please everybody. All you can strive for is to do the best it is humanly possible for you to do." Knowing Marian needed time to regain her balance, Mrs. Anderson suggested she think about some of the other things she might like to do with her life.

Eventually, Marian recovered and took up singing again. She sat down at the piano and sang some of her favorite songs. There was also a pressing practical reason for returning to music. The longer she stayed away from singing, the less income there was for the family. She began going back to Mr. Boghetti's studio on a regular basis to work on her weaknesses.

Since she was now absolutely certain that her weakness with European languages was at the heart of her problem, Marian worked hard to overcome it. Mr. Boghetti had a high school teacher come to his studio to help Marian with her French, and he later arranged special coaching on her French songs by a distinguished bass who sang with the Metropolitan Opera. And, as usual, Mr. Boghetti worked with Marian personally on any music requiring Italian.

However, German was the big problem, and Marian knew that something very drastic had to be done. She even wondered if she should avoid singing German songs completely, but she rejected that idea. She could not expect to have a serious singing career unless she mastered the German *lieder*. Besides, she had loved German songs ever since she began singing them. Although she did not find a German teacher, she did seek out someone who was fluent in German to help her with the pronunciation.

Marian knew very well this could only be a temporary solution. Learning the correct pronunciation and meaning of German words in her songs was not enough. She needed to master the German language so that she could understand it from the inside, and for that she needed to study in Germany. That was out of the question for the time being, but the very fact that she was thinking along these lines showed that her hopes and dreams were coming back.

Soon Marian was singing professionally again. Since she and Billy had kept a card file of all the places they had sung, getting back on the concert circuit was not that difficult. They wrote to all the schools, churches, and organizations they had listed on their cards, and soon the invitations began coming in. With Billy at the piano, Marian was back singing concerts again.

Lewisohn Stadium Contest

In 1925, Marian entered a contest sponsored by the Lewisohn Stadium Concerts in New York City. The prize was to be a guest appearance with the New York Philharmonic Orchestra in the stadium. Mr. Boghetti had encouraged Marian to enter, and he helped her prepare "O mio Fernando," an Italian aria from Donizetti's *La Favorita*. This was to be Marian's major number, but she prepared two other songs just in case the judges wanted to hear something more.

On the day of the trials, Marian took the train to New York, where Mr. Boghetti had a studio. There she and another student, a soprano named Reba Patton, rehearsed their numbers with Mr. Boghetti's studio pianist. Then they all headed over to Aeolian Hall, which was packed with contestants, accompanists, and teachers. Marian was amazed at the huge number of contestants—at least three hundred. Just knowing that she was up against many of the best young professional singers in the country excited her.

Because of the large number of contestants, the organizers used numbers rather than names. Miss Patton was 44, and Marian was 44A, although she was actually about sixtieth in line. All she could do was listen to the other singers and wait her turn.

The judges wanted to hear at least a hundred contestants a day, so they had to be swift with their judgments. They used a loud clicker to inform the contestants that they had made their decision. When it sounded, the contestant had to stop singing and quickly get off the stage to make way for the next contestant. To add to the stress of the occasion, it was a hot, muggy day in New York, and the hall had no air conditioning.

As Marian's turn approached, Mr. Boghetti told her that even if the clicker sounded, she must keep on singing to the end of the aria and be sure to include the trill. Marian had already heard at least six contestants begin singing "O mio Fernando," only to be clicked into silence and sent offstage. Not a single one of them had been allowed to finish the aria. Despite Mr. Boghetti's suggestion, Marian decided that she would abide by the rules of the contest. When the clicker sounded, she would stop singing.

Finally, it was Marian's turn. She took her place on stage and began the aria, half expecting to hear the dreaded clicker at any moment. But as she sang on, the clicker did not sound. Marian sang the aria, including the trill, all the way through to the end. She was the very first contestant the judges allowed to finish. When she stopped, there was a burst of applause from the other contestants. Immediately, an irritated voice came over the loudspeaker to remind everyone about the rule against applause. Then one of the judges called from the balcony, "Does 44A have another song?" Marian sang one of the other songs she had prepared.

Marian knew she had done well, but she had to wait several days for the official word. Then Mr. Boghetti told her the good news—she was one of the sixteen contestants who had been chosen for the semifinals.

Several weeks later, Marian returned to New York for another round, to reduce the sixteen semifinalists to four finalists. Unfortunately, while trying to learn to swim at the YWCA in Philadelphia, Marian's ear had become infected. She told Mr. Boghetti about her earache, but she did not let him know how much it really hurt, because she did not want to alarm him. He was nervous enough as it was. At the semifinals, Marian sang "O mio Fernando" and her two other songs for the judges, and then she and Mr. Boghetti left the hall with no idea if she would make the finals.

By the time they reached Mr. Boghetti's New York studio, Marian's ear was throbbing. All she could think about was getting back to Philadelphia as fast as possible. She barely noticed when the phone rang and Mr. Boghetti went into the other room to answer it. After a short conversation, he rushed back out. "We won!" he shouted. "There will be no finals!"

Marian could not believe it. Mr. Boghetti explained that the judges were so impressed by the quality of Marian's singing and its clear superiority over that of all the other semifinalists that they saw no point in having finals. Marian was naturally thrilled and excited, but by now the pain in her ear was so excruciating that it was hard for her to enjoy the moment. All she wanted to do was to get on that train.

Back in Philadelphia, she went immediately to her doctor, who found that she had a severe abscess. He treated it and then put a dressing on her ear. In the meantime, her family and friends were elated by the news of Marian's victory. By the next day, everybody in Philadelphia seemed to know about Marian winning the contest because all the papers wrote about it.

August 26, 1925, was the big night. Marian went to New York in the morning to rehearse with the New York Philharmonic. She had never sung with an orchestra, but the conductor made her feel relaxed and accepted. Knowing that a large contingent of family, friends, and well-wishers from Philadelphia were taking the train to New York just to hear her sing made Marian feel good, but still a little nervous. There was the lingering memory of the Town Hall disaster, but Marian had been singing for too long and in too many places to let that truly bother her.

That night when it was time for her to sing, Marian walked onto the stage past the members of the orchestra and took her place next to the conductor. She was wearing a new powder-blue dress that she thought was striking without being ostentatious and went well with her dark complexion. When she looked out at the stadium, she saw an endless sea of faces, many of them black. The enthusiastic applause that greeted her before she even began to sing made her feel welcome. She concentrated on the conductor, and at his signal, she sang "O mio Fernando" with great power and feeling. The stadium audience applauded enthusiastically, while the orchestra showed their appreciation by tapping their bows on their music stands. Marian then sang several spirituals.

The reviews the next day were positive but reserved. *The New York Times* said that Marian made "an excellent impression" and "is endowed by nature with a voice of unusual compass, color, and dramatic capacity."[5] *The New York Herald Tribune* spoke of the remarkable strength and naturalness of Marian's voice, but added that "she still has room for further progress."[6]

Marian's appearance at Lewisohn Stadium with the New York Philharmonic gave her career a big boost. When she and Billy resumed their concerts in the fall, there were more and better engagements and Marian's fee rose to $350 and occasionally even to $500. Invitations to sing came from as far away as the West Coast and Canada. Even in the South, the character of Marian's audiences began to change. Now when she gave a concert at a black school or college, there would be white as well as black people in the audience.

Late in her career, when an interviewer asked Marian what was the greatest moment in her life, she answered without hesitation that "it was the day I went home and told my mother she wouldn't need to take work home any more."[7] Marian's mother had worked to support her daughters ever since her husband's death. She had cleaned houses and taken in laundry, and then for many years she had worked full-time as a night cleaning lady at Wanamaker's department store in downtown Philadelphia. Several times Marian had tried unsuccessfully to get her mother to stop working. Finally, when Mrs. Anderson fell ill and had to stay in bed until she could recover and return to work, Marian called the store to say that her mother was ill, adding, "I just wanted to tell you that Mother will not be coming back to work."[8] Marian never felt happier.

Judson Management

As a result of her stadium appearance in 1925, Marian came to the attention of one of the top concert managers in the country, Arthur Judson. When she appeared in Carnegie Hall as a soloist with the Hall Johnson Choir, Mr. Judson went backstage and introduced himself. He told her he thought his office could help her with her career and encouraged her to come in and talk with him about it.

The following week, Marian and Mr. Boghetti met with Mr. Judson in his Philadelphia office. He talked about the higher fees and better bookings he could offer her. Although Marian was disappointed to find out that one of Mr. Judson's assistants, and not Judson himself, would handle her concerts, she thought that her association with the Judson name would be beneficial. After further discussions about the arrangements, and after talking the matter over with Mr. Boghetti, Marian signed a contract with the Arthur Judson people. They asked her to turn over the card file that she and Billy had built, as well as the names of other organizations to which they had sent letters. Marian also agreed to turn over all future concert requests to the Judson office.

For Marian, there were some obvious advantages to having the Judson office manage her concerts. She and Billy no longer had to handle correspondence and negotiate fees. Now she could simply tell people that she was under Judson management and that they should contact George Colledge, who was handling her concerts. He wrote to all the people on Marian's list to inform them that Judson was managing Marian's career and that her singing fee was now $500. Most places agreed to pay the higher fee. The ones who could not afford to do so simply stopped inviting her. Hampton Institute, which regarded Marian as its own pride and joy, was pleased and proud to find out that she was represented by the respected Judson management.

The higher fee did not automatically translate into higher earnings, because Marian had new and unexpected expenses. She had to pay for the four-page leaflets that contained the text of her songs and their English translations, which the Judson office prepared for her audiences. She also had to absorb the cost of other printed matter. In addition, she had to pay Billy King more for his services, and she had to buy more evening dresses.

Marian continued to sing at the same churches and schools, her concerts originating for the most part from the card file she and Billy had built up and turned over to Judson. Eventually, Judson began adding its own engagements, but it took several years for Marian to be directly supervised by Mr. Judson's main office.

Marian had hoped that Judson would help advance her

career, but she was disappointed. As she sang the same concerts year after year, she felt that her career was leveling off and that she was in a rut. She did not think that the Judson office was working very hard for her. She also suspected the office was meeting resistance on the concert circuit since, as a young black singer, she lacked the European reputation that Roland Hayes had. Marian knew that she had to find a way to go to Europe.

Finally she told Mr. Judson that she felt her career was not advancing and that she was thinking about studying abroad. He thought she might really be a soprano rather than a contralto and requested that she sing for a friend, a singer whose opinion he respected. If it turned out that Marian was a soprano after all, Mr. Judson needed to know right away so he would have time to change the billing for the next season. Marian knew she was not a soprano and told him so. It bothered her that her manager had such fundamental doubts about her singing.

Mr. Judson also urged her to study with Frank La Forge, a fine teacher who worked with many famous singers and had many excellent connections. When Marian followed Mr. Judson's advice, problems developed. First of all, Mr. Boghetti was angry at Marian for even thinking of working with another teacher. When Marian tried to arrange to work with both teachers, Mr. Boghetti would have nothing to do with it.

Another problem was that Marian had to go to New York for her lessons with Mr. La Forge, and the cost of the train trip and the fee made the lessons expensive. Mr. La Forge offered to give Marian an hour lesson for the price of a half-hour if Marian could arrive at his New York studio by nine in the morning. Marian accepted the offer, but she had to get up before dawn to arrive in New York on time. She tried this for three or four weeks, but she stopped when she realized the cost of the travel and the lessons was just too much. Then Mr. La Forge happily informed Marian that he found someone who was willing to donate money for a scholarship for Marian to continue her lessons.

Thanks to this scholarship money, Marian worked with Mr. La Forge for over a year, and once she was able to get an afternoon appointment, the traveling to New York was less of a burden. Marian worked with Mr. La Forge especially hard on German *lieder*. After she mastered "Er, der herrlichste von allen"—the second song of Robert Schumann's cycle, *Frauenliebe und Leben*—Mr. La Forge took her to a recording studio where she made a record of it. It was the first time Marian had ever recorded anything in German. She sang the entire cycle in concert later in her career and recorded it as well.

Mr. La Forge was helpful and supportive, and Marian enjoyed working with him. He certainly did not think Marian should transform herself into a soprano, nor did he discourage her when she spoke of wanting to study in Europe. During her time with him, Marian made progress on her German singing, but she knew that German was still her weak point.

One night Marian sang in Mr. La Forge's studio as part of a program he had arranged for his students and their friends. Before a large audience that included many singers, Marian was in the middle of a German *lied* when suddenly she forgot some of the words. She improvised sounds to take their place instead. Marian was terribly embarrassed and upset, although the others were very understanding about the lapse. The incident, which echoed her Town Hall disaster, haunted Marian for many weeks afterward. Now she was more convinced than ever that she had to study abroad.

When Marian finally informed Mr. Judson that she was determined to go to Europe, he did not hide his disapproval. "If you go to Europe," he told her, "it will only be to satisfy your own vanity."

"Well, then," she said, "let's say that is the reason."[9]

CHAPTER 3

Europe

To a black American artist of the early decades of the twentieth century, Europe offered an opportunity for greater professional advancement. Segregated by law in the South and by practice in the North, America was still a land where blacks were forced to live separate but unequal lives. In white America, black talent in music, art, and sports remained confined to the black community. For talented blacks in any field, America was not yet the land of full opportunity.

For a long time, Marian had known that her career needed a boost. Not only did she need to master the European languages, but she also knew that singing in Europe would afford her the same kind of exposure and credentials that had helped Roland Hayes.

Money had always been the main problem, of course, but Marian's higher fees allowed her to save some money. As usual, Marian discussed this important decision with her mother, who was her confidante and best friend. Her mother encouraged her to go to Europe, as did her sisters and her friends at the church.

England

Marian bought a second-class ticket on the old *Ile de France* and set sail for England. She had the names of two people to contact for help and advice. Billy King, who was as enthusiastic about her going as Marian was, had given her a letter of introduction to Roger Quilter, an Englishman who had befriended Roland Hayes. Billy had written to Mr. Quilter about Marian, and he had indicated that he would be willing to help her when she reached London. Roland Hayes's accompanist, Lawrence Brown, had also written on Marian's behalf to Raimund von Zur Mühlen, a highly respected teacher of German *lieder* in England.

Even though Marian was alone for most of the voyage across the Atlantic, she was so excited that the time went quickly. One evening while strolling on deck, she got the chance to try out her high school French when a Frenchman started up a conversation. Marian attempted to say something in her halting French about the full moon, calling it *le soleil*, much to the amusement of the Frenchman. When Marian realized her mistake (*soleil* means "sun"), she excused herself and went below.

After the ship docked in Southampton, England, Marian took the boat train to London, where she arrived at Paddington Station late at night. She found a phone booth and called Roger Quilter. The butler who answered the phone told her that Mr. Quilter was in a nursing home.

Marian's heart sank. There she was, stranded late at night in a strange city with her bag, music case, purse, two coats, and nowhere to go. She remembered that the black actor, John Payne, who had once visited the Andersons in Philadelphia, lived in London somewhere. Originally a member of an American black theater group that played in London, he liked the city so much that he decided to leave the group and settle in London. Marian remembered that he had once told Marian's family that he hoped they would visit him and his wife if they were ever in London, but that had been a long time ago.

Marian looked his name up in the telephone directory and called. She was greatly relieved that he was home, and that he remembered her well. After she told him about her predicament, he insisted that she stay in the couple's spare room. Feeling much better, Marian gathered up her belongings and took a cab to John Payne's house on Regent's Park

Road. The Paynes greeted her warmly and made her feel right at home. They had a long conversation, but as the Paynes prepared to show Marian to her room, she discovered her music case was missing.

The Paynes guessed that she had left it in the cab, so they asked her if she remembered the cab or the driver. Marian told them that the cab was distinctive because it did not have a back window, but John Payne informed her that most English cabs didn't have a back window. He suggested that Marian get some sleep, and they would look for the case in the morning.

Marian stayed awake, trying to retrace her steps and remember where she had the case last. All of her books and personal papers were in the case, along with traveler's checks and a letter of credit for a thousand dollars. That was all the money she had, except for a few dollars' worth of English money she had exchanged in Southampton.

The next day John Payne took Marian to Scotland Yard to report the loss of the case and to see if any information about it had turned up. They also reported the loss of her letter of credit at the bank where it was drawn and the loss of her traveler's checks at American Express.

Marian thought the porter who had helped her at the train station might be able to help her find the right taxi driver, so after dinner that night, she and Mrs. Payne went back to Paddington Station where the station master let them walk up and down the platforms looking for the porter. When they told a policeman their problem, he suggested they try the station's Lost Property Office. As soon as Marian began telling her story to the man behind the desk, he disappeared behind a partition and came back with Marian's music case.

"That's my case!" said Marian excitedly. Before the man would turn the case over to her, Marian had to describe the contents and sign a ledger. A policeman had found the case in the phone booth and turned it in to the Lost Property Office. Marian tipped both men—the man behind the desk and the policeman. She returned to the Paynes happily clutching her case.

A few days later, Marian called Raimund von Zur Mühlen, the man Lawrence Brown had recommended as the leading teacher of German *lieder* in England. She made an appointment to sing for him at his home in the small town of Steyning in Sussex, about fifty miles south of London.

When Marian arrived at the home of von Zur Mühlen— or "Master," as everybody called him—she felt apprehensive. A maid showed her into a large room with a piano at one end and Master at the other. Because he was elderly and not well, he sat in a chair with a red blanket over his knees. He pounded his cane on the floor whenever he wanted to get somebody's attention. A young accompanist entered the room and went over to the piano. Marian gave the accompanist the music for one of her very favorite German *lieder*, "Im Abendrot." After he played the introduction, Marian closed her eyes and sang. When she finished, there was a long silence.

"Come here," said Master from the other end of the room. Marian took the long walk across the room, wondering what he was going to say.

"Do you know what that song means?" he asked. Marian admitted that she did not know the meaning of every single word.

"Don't sing it if you don't know what it's about," he said rather bluntly.

"I know what it's about," said Marian, "but I don't know it word for word."

"That's not enough."

He asked her to sing something she knew about. Marian sang "My Lord, What a Morning," one of her favorite spirituals. She had learned it in church as a little girl and had been singing it ever since.

Before she finished, Master pounded his cane on the floor. Marian wondered, What now?

"Wait a minute!" he shouted across the room. "You're singing like a queen, and I have not crowned you yet."

Marian made arrangements to live in the home of a young printer and his wife, so that she could study with Master on a regular basis. He lent Marian his book of Schubert songs and suggested she learn the first one, "Nähe des Geliebten." The German text had no English translation, so Marian had to get help with the meaning and pronunciation of the German words from the printer and a friend of his, who knew German.

Unfortunately, Marian had had only two lessons with Master when he became seriously ill. Marian stayed in Steyning for several weeks in the hope that he would recover, but then she returned to the Paynes in London. When she called to find out how Master was, she was disappointed to hear that his condition was worse and that he would have to stop all his teaching for the foreseeable future. Marian was crushed, because after only two lessons, she was convinced that Master was the answer to her most pressing artistic problems.

Needing to find a new teacher, she called Roger Quilter, who was back home and feeling better. He was eager to help Marian in any way he could. On his recommendation, Marian studied with Mark Raphael, who specialized in German *lieder* and had himself studied with Master. He proved to be a good teacher, although Marian was still disappointed about not having the chance to study with Master.

Marian lived with the Paynes while she worked on her music. She did not go out in London much because she wanted to save her money. To see more of the city, she occasionally rode a bus to the end of the line and then back. She attended a few concerts, hearing the pianist Arthur Rubinstein and several notable singers, including Lily Pons. On Sundays, the Paynes invited musicians, artists, and actors to their house, so Marian met interesting people.

Roger Quilter was also immensely helpful. His large

house was a gathering place for composers, musicians, and society people from all over England, and often he asked Marian to sing for his guests. Once she sang a full program of songs in German, Italian, and English, including several by Mr. Quilter. The listeners liked Marian's voice so much that they talked her into giving a recital at Wigmore Hall— what proved to be her first European concert. Mr. Quilter and his friends also arranged an appearance for her at one of the Promenade Concerts under the direction of Sir Henry Wood. However, most of Marian's time in London was spent as a student rather than as a performer.

When Marian returned to the United States, she was glad to see her family and friends and resume her new season of Judson concerts. In the fall of 1930, Marian gave nineteen concerts in all, not as many as she used to sing when she and Billy were doing their own bookings. Before long, that old feeling that her career was standing still returned. Marian wanted to find a way to get back to Europe, but this time she wanted to go to Germany. She was determined to learn German so that she could finally sing *lieder* the way they were meant to be sung.

Germany

Marian sang a concert in Chicago for the Alpha Kappa Alpha sorority, which had made her an honorary member. A man came backstage after the concert and introduced himself as a representative of the Julius Rosenwald Fund, which had been established by a wealthy Chicago businessman to help blacks advance their education. He asked Marian about her background and plans, and when she spoke of her desire to study in Germany, he encouraged her to apply for a fellowship.

Marian visited the office of the Rosenwald Fund and filled out a fellowship application. She was assured that funding was available, and she went ahead with her preparations to go to Germany. However, because of her concert commitments with Judson, she wrote the Rosenwald Fund office to tell them that she wanted the fellowship for six months rather than a year.

Two days before she was to leave, Marian received a letter from the Rosenwald Fund telling her the fellowship had to be for a year. With her trunk packed and waiting in the hallway of the Anderson home, Marian wired the Rosenwald office in Chicago that if she couldn't go for six months, she would not be able to go at all. A few hours later, a telegram came telling her that an exception was being made in her case. Marian picked up the fellowship money the next day, and by the following evening, she was on a German steamship at a New York pier ready to set sail for Europe.

Germany was much harder to get used to than England. Marian did not know a single person in the country, and from the moment she got off the train in Berlin, she was surrounded by strangers speaking a language she did not understand. The Judson office had arranged for a concert manager by the name of Mr. Walter to meet Marian at the station, but nobody showed up. When Marian tried to make her way downstairs from the platform to the street, a uniformed guard blocked her way. Despite a smattering of words she had picked up in London when she took some German lessons, Marian was not able to make herself understood. Only by inching around to the other side and blending in with the next group of train passengers that surged toward the stairs was she able to get past the guard.

Down in the station itself, she clutched her music case tightly, determined not to lose it again. She wandered around looking for somebody who spoke English until she found a travel desk where they made a reservation for her at a hotel on the outskirts of the city. Marian took a taxi to the hotel where she was booked into a large, clean room. She went to bed but could not sleep. She had missed the connection with the manager who was supposed to meet her, and now she had no idea how to contact him. She lay in bed trying to figure out what she should do the next day.

In the morning, the hotel clerk helped her place a call to a man she knew only as Mr. Walter. She asked him to come and meet her in the lobby of the hotel. When two men showed up, Marian figured the second man was Mr. Walter's assistant.

"Guten tag," Marian said and then told them she was Marian Anderson.

The men looked at each other blankly. The name obviously meant nothing to them.

"Judson," said Marian, pronouncing the magic word with great care.

"Judson?" The men looked at each other again and shrugged their shoulders. They were polite, but after several minutes of a rather strained conversation in broken English, they asked the hotel clerk to translate for them. Soon the difficulty was straightened out and the men left. Marian had called the wrong number, and the two men were in a business that had nothing to do with music. With the help of the clerk again, Marian finally tracked down the right Mr. Walter.

Mr. Walter arranged for Marian to rent a room in the apartment of an elderly German couple. Herr von Edburg, who was a semiretired actor, knew a little English, but Frau von Edburg spoke no English at all. With the help of Marian's pocket dictionary and lots of gestures and sounds, they somehow managed to communicate. In this environment, Marian now had to learn German.

She bought a language book, and Herr von Edburg helped her with the lessons. Every day they pored over the book, taking turns reading the German. There was an English translation on the opposite page, but Herr von Edburg insisted that Marian not look at it. The lessons were painstakingly slow but effective.

When Marian began voice lessons with Michael Rau-cheisen, a highly recommended teacher, she felt more comfortable than she ever had with the words of the German *lieder*. The more she studied German and heard it spoken, the more she felt herself understanding the nuances and the deeper meanings of the words.

In October 1930, Marian gave a recital at the Bachsaal, a famous Berlin concert hall named after Johann Sebastian Bach. She had to put up her own money to give the recital, but she was willing to sacrifice part of her fellowship money for the chance to sing before a German audience. After all, singing well and receiving good reviews for a performance in front of a German audience that knew the words of German *lieder* by heart would be a real accomplishment.

Michael Raucheisen, who was Marian's accompanist for the recital, was so nervous that Marian did not have time to worry about herself. His mother was as nervous as he was. Marian was amused when Frau Raucheisen came backstage before the recital, not to wish Marian good luck with her Berlin debut, but to comfort her son.

Marian was curious about how many people would show up, perhaps remembering the disappointment she had felt when she looked out on the sparse audience that attended her Town Hall concert. She also wondered how it would feel singing to an audience that knew all the songs better than she did. "It gave me a strange feeling," she said later.

When Marian went out on the stage to give her first recital in Germany, she was pleasantly surprised to find that the Bachsaal was full. She began her recital with a series of songs by Beethoven, which she had never sung in public before. There was no reaction after the first song, but as she proceeded, she felt the interest of the audience growing. By the end of the Beethoven series, Marian knew that the audience was very receptive to her singing. Before the recital, Michael Raucheisen had been so nervous that he had not uttered a word, but when they left the stage after the Bee-thoven songs, he said, "Didn't I tell you it was going to be fine?"

Marian was more confident about the rest of the pro-gram. When she came back on stage, she sang a group of Schubert songs that she had been singing for years. The au-dience applauded vigorously, forcing her to return to the stage for a bow, first with her accompanist and then by her-self. After the intermission, Marian sang songs in English, including spirituals, and the audience showed its appreciation by applauding warmly. After the recital, many Germans came backstage to tell Marian how much they enjoyed her singing, and some even asked for her autograph.

Marian's feeling of triumph was short-lived, however, because the next day she could not find one newspaper that even mentioned the recital. The manager had stressed how important it was to get reviewed, so Marian was naturally puzzled and disappointed. Had the critics not attended, or had they simply decided that the recital didn't deserve cov-erage? Marian began to wonder if her German had been good enough.

Marian finally told Herr von Edburg about her disap-pointment at not being reviewed. He said not to worry; Ber-lin critics never rushed into print, and it took a week or two for reviews to appear. He turned out to be right. The critics took their time, but when the reviews finally came out, they were favorable.

The recital was noticed as far away as Stockholm, Swe-den, by Helmert Enwall, the director of Konsertbolaget, Scandinavia's largest concert management. Since Director Enwall, as he was called, was always looking for new talent, he wanted to find out more about this young black singer from America. He thought her name would help her in Swe-den, where Anderson is a very common name. Enwall sent two of his associates to Berlin to find out more about this

Marian Anderson and to see if she might be interested in performing in Scandinavia.

One day when Marian was in the middle of her lesson with Mr. Raucheisen, two men whom she had never seen before entered the studio. They spoke to Raucheisen, who introduced them to Marian. One of the men was Rulle Rasmussen, a concert manager from Norway, and the other was Kosti Vehanen, a Finnish pianist. They told her Director Enwall was looking for new talent and might be interested in having her sing some concerts in Scandinavia. They asked her if they could hear her sing, so Marian invited them to the recital she was giving that very evening.

That night in the former palace of the kaiser, the two men listened intently to Marian sing a program that happened to consist entirely of spirituals. Although neither man was familiar with that kind of music, they could hear the power and range of Marian's voice. They approached Marian after the recital. Mr. Rasmussen told her she would definitely be hearing from him. He said he could not speak for Director Enwall, but he knew he wanted her to perform in Norway and said that he was going to go back home and see about the arrangements. Kosti Vehanen was equally impressed. When he returned to Stockholm, he reported favorably to Director Enwall about Marian's voice.

A few weeks later, Mr. Rasmussen wrote to Marian to say that everything had been arranged. She would appear in Oslo, Stockholm, and Helsinki, singing one recital in each city and a second one if the first was successful.

Scandinavia

Marian's first scheduled recital was in Oslo, but on the way Mr. Rasmussen decided that she should sing in the city of Stavanger. Marian's debut in Scandinavia went so well that Mr. Rasmussen scheduled an additional recital in Bergen on the southwestern coast of Norway. When Marian sang in the Norwegian capital of Oslo, the response was so enthusiastic that a second recital was immediately scheduled and sold out.

Everywhere Marian went in Norway, the audiences loved her. At the end of the first half of her first recital in Oslo, the applause was so prolonged that it was difficult to stop it for the intermission. Norwegians who spoke English kept calling Marian at her hotel, and many came to her in person to bring flowers or just to talk—about Norway, about America, about music, about the problems blacks faced in the United States.

Norway was not used to blacks, so people were both curious and open-minded. On the street, strangers followed Marian, some of them passing and then turning around just so they could walk past her and smile. Marian did not take offense because she knew they were just trying to be friendly.

Newspapers were also curious. One concert review reported that Marian was "dressed in electric-blue satin and looking very much like a chocolate bar." Another review compared her color to café au lait. Marian was not upset because she knew no harm was intended. "The comments had nothing to do with any prejudice," she said, "they expressed a kind of wonder."[1]

In Sweden, Director Enwall handled Marian's concerts directly. He prepared carefully for the first one, still believing that the name Anderson would attract attention, especially since it was obvious that Marian wasn't Swedish. The first recital went well enough for there to be a second, and that one was sold out, but the Swedes did not respond as enthusiastically as the Norwegians had. Marian was a little puzzled by the reserve she encountered in Sweden, but Director Enwall told her that this was a national trait. The Swedes, he said, are slow to show warmth, but when they do, it is strong and lasting.

Marian liked the Enwalls enormously and became close friends with Mrs. Enwall. Since in those days Marian did not have much of a wardrobe, Mrs. Enwall took her shopping so she would not have to wear the same blue satin dress for every concert. Mrs. Enwall persuaded Marian to buy a fashionable white crepe dress with a long train. However, Marian felt so self-conscious about the train that she had it cut off.

Helsinki was Kosti Vehanen's home, so when Marian sang in the Finnish capital with Kosti as her accompanist, there was a special atmosphere. Kosti's friends and family helped make Marian feel especially welcome. The response of the Finns to Marian's two recitals was so enthusiastic that Marian knew immediately that she wanted to return to Finland as often as she could. She even sang a very simple folk song in Finnish that Kosti taught her, which the audience greatly appreciated.

Beginning with Helsinki, Kosti became Marian's regular accompanist in what proved to be a long and fortunate association for both of them. Kosti was a talented, well-trained musician who had accompanied many accomplished singers, including the American contralto, Madame Charles Cahier, who was very popular in Europe. Kosti was also a linguist and a man of education and culture. Having studied in Germany, he was fluent in German, so he was a great help to Marian when they worked on *lieder* together. "It is not too much to say," Marian said later about him, "that he helped me a great deal in guiding me onto the path that led to my becoming an accepted international singer."[2]

Kosti remembered what Marian sounded like when he sat down with her for their very first rehearsal: "It was as though the room had begun to vibrate . . . the very atmosphere was charged with beauty—certainly the tone must come from under the earth. . . . the sound I heard swelled to majestic power . . . and I was enthralled by one of nature's rare wonders."[3]

After Marian's highly successful concerts in Helsinki, she and Kosti returned to Stockholm to give another recital before proceeding on to Copenhagen. Denmark was another country where Marian felt immediately at home. News of her earlier successes had preceded her, so the Copenhagen audiences were larger from the start. Once again, people went out of their way to seek Marian out to show their appreciation. They visited her in her hotel, invited her to their homes, and sent her flowers and notes.

Marian could not get over the way the Scandinavians accepted her as an individual and judged her as a human being and as a singer on the basis of her character and talent rather than the color of her skin. How different it was from back home where the laws of segregation always reminded Marian of her skin color, where restaurants refused to serve her because she was black, and where hotels, *if* they accepted her, told her not to invite black friends to visit.

In Scandinavia, Marian felt that people perceived and judged her differently. "They accepted you as an individual in your own right, judging you for your qualities as a human being and artist and for nothing else," she said. "Even the first curiosity about my outward difference was in no way disturbing or offensive, and it seemed only a moment before that dropped away."[4]

Marian's concert fees on this first Scandinavian tour were modest, but the experience was invaluable. The tour, with its appreciative audiences and warm personal contacts, strengthened Marian's confidence and energized her ambition. All the hard work she had put in over the years seemed to be paying off, and now all her hopes and dreams seemed within reach. The wonderful confirmation of her ability that Scandinavian audiences gave her meant that Marian was willing to sing with more spontaneity and emotional freedom. "I know I felt that this acceptance provided the basis for daring to pour out reserves of feeling I had not called upon."[5]

At the end of Marian's six months in Europe, she returned home for another Judson concert season. Bits of news about Marian's success in Scandinavia had trickled back to the United States, but it made no difference. Marian found that the Judson office had booked her into the same schools, churches, and halls.

At the beginning of her Judson tour in 1932, Marian received a cable from Director Enwall in Stockholm promising her twenty concerts if she returned to Scandinavia. This cable was soon followed by a second, promising her forty concerts. No sooner had Marian replied, explaining that she was committed to her American tour, then she received yet another cable promising *sixty* concerts. Marian honored her American commitments, but she applied for the second half of the Rosenwald Fund fellowship. She received it, and after she finished her Judson tour, she returned to Europe where she remained for more than two years.

During the next year, 1933–34, the enthusiasm for Marian's singing was so contagious that she sang all over Scandinavia, even in remote towns in the frozen north, sometimes two or three concerts in the same town. By the time she left Scandinavia, she had sung 116 concerts!

The halls in which Marian sang were always packed, and the audiences were enthusiastic. Scandinavian newspapers were full of Marian's picture and articles about her life and her career. Even the restrained Swedes fell in love with Marian and embraced her wholeheartedly. One newspaper described the whole phenomenon as "Marian fever."

Except for a few pieces by Edvard Grieg, Marian had not sung Scandinavian songs in America, but with Kosti's encouragement she studied Scandinavian music and sang in the language of her audience. Kosti introduced Marian to the songs of the great Finnish composer, Jean Sibelius, and he taught her Swedish folk songs. Scandinavian audiences were especially moved when they learned that Marian had taken the trouble to learn their songs.

The Sibelius song that intrigued Marian the most was "Norden," and when she sang it in Helsinki, the audience responded with thunderous applause. Kosti was so excited by the response that he called Sibelius, whom he knew, and asked him if Marian could come and sing for him. The seventy-year-old composer agreed and invited them to his home in the country.

On the appointed day, Marian and Kosti drove to the composer's villa deep in the forest northwest of Helsinki. Kosti told Marian that they would have only half an hour, time enough for a couple of songs and a cup of coffee. When they arrived, Sibelius and his wife greeted them warmly. Sibelius was shorter than Marian had imagined, but with his broad shoulders and head he looked like a figure "chiseled out of granite." The composer asked Marian if she wanted some coffee, but Kosti thought it would be better for Marian's voice if she sang first. Kosti was even more nervous than Marian about how Sibelius would receive her songs.

The two Sibelius songs Marian sang were "Aus banger Brust" and "Sländan." Kosti remembered being struck by how calm and confident Marian was and how superb her voice sounded. When she finished, Sibelius went to the door and told his wife, "Not coffee, but champagne!" Then he went to Marian and embraced her. He told her, "My ceiling is much too low for your voice."[6]

Marian was overwhelmed, and Kosti beamed with pride. Sitting around a table with Kosti as interpreter, they talked about music, with the composer sometimes going to the piano to make certain points. His only suggestion to Marian about singing his songs was "more Anderson and less Sibelius." Mrs. Sibelius, who was a charming, friendly woman, asked Marian about her home and family. Marian was only too happy to talk about her mother and sisters.

The visit lasted much longer than the scheduled half-hour. Marian felt blessed for the chance to meet the great composer, and Kosti described the meeting as "one of the most precious moments in our lives." Afterward, every time Marian sang a Sibelius song, she felt she had a special, very personal insight into his music. "It was as if a veil had been lifted,"[7] she said.

After their meeting, Sibelius took a special interest in Marian's singing and even traveled to Helsinki to attend one of her recitals. Years later, when Marian returned to Helsinki, Sibelius sent her a telegram welcoming her back to Finland. Marian and Kosti also visited the young Finnish composer Yrjö Kilpinen, whose songs Marian also sang in concert. In Denmark, Marian met Edvard Grieg's widow, who was so pleased that Marian sang one of her husband's songs in Norwegian that she invited Marian to tea.

This second, more extended tour of Scandinavia was a wonderful period in Marian's life. People loved her, her reputation grew, and her earnings allowed her to send money home and expand her own concert wardrobe. She bought new evening gowns, street clothes, luggage, and gifts for friends like the Enwalls. They were like family, and she stayed for long periods in their home. Marian was also finally able to buy the music she needed, and she could even afford to have it bound in leather.

As Marian's long Scandinavian tour came to an end, Director Enwall urged her to remain in Europe rather than return to the United States. He wanted Marian to sing in London, Paris, and other important centers of European music. He had written to important concert managements in other cities about Marian and had been encouraged by their interest.

Having been acclaimed by Scandinavia's most important musicians and critics to a degree that had never happened in her own country, and now being offered a chance to sing in London and Paris, Marian did not need much persuading. She wrote to the Judson office and asked them to postpone her engagements. The office had booked only ten concerts for the coming season, and they were no improvement over the concerts she had been singing for years. Nonetheless, they informed her that they could not postpone the concerts.

Marian now faced one of her most important decisions. Despite her dissatisfaction with their management, the Judson organization was Marian's only professional tie with her own country. Yet she also knew how important it was to sing in Europe. Marian made her decision. She wrote the Judson office and told them to cancel the season's concerts. She was staying in Europe and set no date for returning to the United States. In effect, Marian was burning her American bridges behind her. It was a strange feeling—and a little scary.

London and Paris

Marian felt quite at home in London, because she had already lived there. She was glad to see the Paynes again, and she paid a visit to her old friend, Roger Quilter.

Director Enwall, who was now serving as Marian's general European manager, had tried to get London's biggest agency to represent Marian, but it had not been sufficiently impressed by her credentials. He had then enlisted a smaller agency to make the arrangements for a recital. Marian sang well, but the hall was too small and the concert was not sufficiently advertised. The reviews, which were reserved and brief, were evidence that the English did not respond to Marian's singing the way the Scandinavians did.

Marian missed her mother terribly, so it was a great occasion in 1934 when she finally persuaded Mrs. Anderson to visit her in Europe. When Marian's mother arrived in Le Havre, France, Marian was there at the pier to meet her.

In May 1934, Marian gave her first Paris recital in the Salle Gaveau. Although the concert was not well attended, the enthusiasm of the audience led to a second performance, which was sold out. When Marian's Paris manager, Mr. Fritz Horowitz, proposed a third concert, Marian hesitated. It was already June, and she wondered if three successive concerts in the same city was a good idea. The Enwalls, who had come to hear Marian's Paris debut, had already returned to Sweden, so Marian did not have the benefit of their advice.

Mr. Horowitz said there was great demand for another

concert, so Marian agreed. When he proved his point by selling all the tickets, Marian was relieved. Her program that night, which showed off her great versatility, included Schubert's "Bird Song," an aria from a French opera, an ancient lullaby, a lively sailor song written by Kosti, and the spirituals with which she usually closed her concerts. The audience loved Marian's singing and so did the critics. Marian's third Paris concert was such a great success that she felt she was now really on her way.

That concert in June 1934 turned out to be very important for another reason. During the intermission, a short, balding man wearing horn-rimmed glasses appeared backstage and introduced himself. As soon as she heard his name—Sol Hurok—she knew he was the internationally known American concert manager.

That afternoon, Mr. Hurok had been sitting at a sidewalk café with his wife and friends when he spotted a half-hidden poster advertising a recital that night by "an American contralto." He told his wife, "I think I'll just look in."

In his memoirs, Sol Hurok wrote that "chills danced up my spine and my palms were wet" when he saw "a tall, handsome Negro girl" come out on stage that night walking "with the grace of a queen." He described his reaction to her voice:

> I was shaken to my very shoes. Ten years ago her voice was not the finished, the polished instrument it is today. But the same great heart was behind it, the same deep love and understanding for music as a language of the human spirit . . . anyone who had ears to hear her then could hear the great future already present.[8]

Mr. Hurok wasted no time letting Marian know what was on his mind. "I want to present you in your own country," he told her and suggested they all meet in Mr. Horowitz's office the next day.

When Marian and Kosti went to Mr. Horowitz's office,

Mr. Hurok, with "the impressive bulk befitting the grand impresario," was sitting behind the desk with Mr. Horowitz at his side. Marian already knew that Sol Hurok was a man who took risks for the artists he believed in and stood up for them, whatever the odds.

Mr. Hurok asked many questions. What sort of arrangement did Marian have with Judson? How many concerts had she sung in the United States each season? How much had she been paid? He did not mention the concert the night before, but he finally got around to saying what Marian most wanted to hear: "I might be able to do something for you."

He told Marian he could guarantee fifteen concerts, and that she would be able to count on a down payment before the tour began. Marian liked the idea, but she told him that she could not discuss a contract with him until the Judson office released her, even though she had not signed a contract with them. He nodded and urged her to cable them. "I was impressed with her concern for perfect correctness in her relations with a manager whom she had in effect already left,"[9] he wrote later.

Afterward, when Kosti insisted that they go to a café and celebrate with a cool drink, Marian agreed. After all the excitement of the meeting and the concert the night before, she felt "like a marathon runner at the end of his race."

Judson did not answer her cable or two letters immediately, but she finally got a letter from one of the staff saying they were sorry to lose her. They had no objection to her signing with another manager if that was what she wanted. A few days later when the details were worked out, Marian signed a contract with Mr. Hurok. It was agreed that Marian would return to the United States in December of the following year. By then, Mr. Hurok would have had time to book her first concerts.

In the meantime, news of Marian's Paris triumph spread, and offers poured in from all over Europe—Belgium, Holland, Italy, Spain, Austria, Hungary, Switzerland, Poland, the Baltic countries, and the Soviet Union. Marian's schedule for the rest of her time in Europe quickly filled in.

When Hitler came to power in Germany in 1933, Marian was establishing her reputation in Scandinavia. The Germans heard about the popularity of this Marian Anderson in Scandinavia, but they obviously did not know who this singer with the nice Swedish name really was, because they kept inviting her to Nazi Germany to sing. Marian's manager answered that she was too busy, or that a trip to Germany could not be worked into her schedule, but the Germans persisted. When they heard that Marian was going to be in Poland, they invited her to come to Berlin. Marian's manager wrote to inquire about the fee, and the Germans indicated their interest. However, before they invited her to sing, they had just one question—was Marian Anderson 100 percent Aryan? That ended the correspondence.

Marian's mother remained in Paris for two months. She was homesick for her daughters and grandson, and she was sure she was in the way. She did not feel she could be of any more help to Marian, who now had so many places to go and so much to do. Mrs. Anderson returned to Philadelphia while Marian continued her European tour.

Austria

Going to Vienna in the spring of 1935 was an emotional experience for Marian because the city had such a rich musical history. So many of the great composers—Mozart, Beethoven, Brahms, Haydn, and Marian's beloved Schubert, whose songs had become "an inextricable part of my life and career"—had made the city their home at some time in their lives. Marian visited the places that had figured in the lives and memories of the great composers, and she felt a special thrill to be able to sing in their city.

Marian's concert took place on March 9, 1935, in the Wiener Konzerthaus, a building that housed two halls, a smaller hall where Marian sang and a larger main hall for major events. Because Marian was a newcomer, her audience was small. However, something very strange happened during the intermission. When Marian returned to sing the second half of her program, the hall was full. Later she found out what had happened. There was a concert going on in the main hall at the same time, and the audiences of the two concerts had mingled during the intermission. The people who had heard Marian spoke so enthusiastically about her that many of the people left the other concert and went to hear the last half of Marian's performance.

The sight of this suddenly enlarged audience moved Marian and inspired her audience as well, giving the second half of her concert a highly charged intensity. When Marian's singing of Bach's "Komm', susser Tod" caused many in the audience to weep openly, Marian knew that she was reaching a new, important level of performance. Years later, she wrote that "there are things in the heart that must enrich the songs I sing. If this does not happen—and it does not always happen—the performance is not fulfilled. With 'Komm', susser Tod' I had probably found the key to the heart. And the audience knew. You cannot fool an audience."[10]

The second concert, which was scheduled immediately, was also enthusiastically received. Herbert F. Peyser, a *New York Times* music critic who was in Europe at the time, wrote that "a sensation of the Vienna music season, and to date perhaps its most dramatic event, has been the debut here of the contralto from Philadelphia, Marian Anderson." Describing the rhapsodic reaction of the press to Marian's two concerts, he said " 'stunning' . . . and 'phenomenal' are the weakest adjectives in currency." Peyser's article, which did a great deal to spread the word about Marian back in the United States, concluded:

There can be no question that Miss Anderson, alike by virtue of her great, gorgeous voice, her art of song, the emotional, indeed the spiritual and mystical elements of her nature that repeatedly lend her work the character of a consecration, her dignity, sympathy, and ineffable sincerity of approach, ranks today among the few imposing vocal confrontations of the age. It is by no means impossible to pick flaws in her work, to cavil at this trifle or that. To do so, however, is a good deal like criticizing the pyramids of Egypt because here and there is a stone crumbled or misshapen."[11]

Marian next went to Salzburg, the beautiful city in the Austrian Alps that was the gathering place every summer of the world's most accomplished musicians, who met there for the Salzburg Music Festival. Marian's first recital was in the Mozarteum, named for Wolfgang Amadeus Mozart. Because she was not yet well known in Austria, her audience was small. However, once again those who heard her spread the word of Marian's artistry through the festival. Soon everybody was talking about the young American contralto, Marian Anderson.

Since so few people had gotten a chance to hear Marian sing, an American woman, Mrs. Gertrude Moulton, a great lover of music, arranged a private recital for Marian in the ballroom of a local hotel. Feeling that Marian should receive wider exposure, now that the city was talking about her, Mrs. Moulton invited many leading musicians and dignitaries. As Marian was getting ready for her recital, she heard a rumor that the great conductor Arturo Toscanini might attend, but she did not believe it. In fact, she half hoped he wouldn't because, she said, "I held him in such high esteem that I felt I could not possibly do anything of interest to him."[12]

Just about every leading light in the world of music who was at the festival that summer—including the conductor Bruno Walter and the great German singer, Lotte Lehmann—showed up at the recital to find out if what was being said about the young black American singer was true. Even the

Catholic Archbishop of Salzburg attended. Just before Marian began her recital, she was informed that Maestro Toscanini was also in the audience.

Marian's program—some Schubert songs, Brahms's "Die Mainacht," and several spirituals—made a great impression on the audience. A writer who was in attendance wrote that "her rapt and trancelike absorption in her music; her dark, angular beauty, all made the experience unlike any other. . . . A mantle of tragedy—that of an individual, of a race, of a destiny—seemed to envelop this artist and set her apart from all others." After Marian finished her final song, "Crucifixion," there was "an electrical silence. I was myself paralyzed and could not have applauded if I had wished to do so. . . . Everybody else was in the same condition."[13]

After the recital, Toscanini, Walter, and many other musicians came backstage to congratulate Marian and thank her for her performance. At the reception afterward, more people crowded around Marian to thank her and say flattering things about her singing. The great Toscanini himself told Madame Cahier, "What I heard today one is privileged to hear only once in a hundred years."

The recital was a complete success, and word quickly spread about what Toscanini had said. Since he was one of the most respected musical figures in the world and the dominant personality at the festival, his extraordinary praise for a little known American singer carried great weight and spread rapidly. Marian was surprised and delighted, but when she found out that his words, spoken in a private conversation, were circulating in public without his permission, she worried that he might think she was somehow taking advantage of his goodwill. "If it had been up to me," she later wrote, "I would not have allowed his comment to be made public."[14] But public it became. It was as if Marian had been anointed by the king of classical music.

As Marian continued touring Europe, she was applauded, praised, and honored everywhere she went. In

Rome she sang in the royal palace, and in Geneva the city fathers honored her at a special dinner. She was already well on her way to becoming a celebrity in Europe.

Soviet Union

Marian made two trips to the Soviet Union that gave her an opportunity, given few Americans, to travel extensively in the new Soviet state, which at that time was less than twenty years old. Kosti had been to Leningrad and Moscow before the Bolshevik Revolution, but he "was eager to see the change that had taken place in this huge, mysterious, half-Oriental country under the Soviets."[15]

Marian's first concert tour of the Soviet Union, in the late fall of 1934, consisted of six concerts, three each in Leningrad and Moscow. Marian remembered how bitter cold it was when she and Kosti got off the train at the border between Finland and the Soviet Union. The snow was piled high, and just walking from the train to the customs shed burned Marian's eyes and froze the hair in her nostrils.

In Leningrad, where it was just as cold, a young Russian woman came to Marian's hotel room to obtain a copy of her program so that she could have the text of the songs translated into Russian for those attending the concert. Marian had been warned that the Soviets would not permit the singing of any religious songs, but she decided she wanted to sing the same kind of songs she sang everywhere else. She had put the Schubert "Ave Maria" and four spirituals on her program, but that did not seem to bother the young woman.

The first Russian concert was packed, as were all five that followed. Before the concert started, the young woman who had come to the hotel addressed the audience. She told them the names of the Italian songs Marian would be singing in the first group and then translated their titles into Russian. After Marian sang the songs, the young woman announced the next group, which began with the German *lieder* and concluded with the "Ave Maria." The young woman referred to it simply as "an aria by Schubert," without naming it.

When it came time for the spirituals, the young woman gave their titles but did not mention their religious content. After singing the spirituals, Marian and Kosti left the stage, assuming the concert was over. As they walked back to the artist's room, they heard a strange swelling noise that grew so loud that it sounded as if the building was falling down. Marian asked Kosti, "What on earth is going on?" but he was as puzzled as she.

The young woman then came into the room and told them that the audience wanted them back on stage. When Marian returned, she saw throngs of Russians pressed up against the stage. They had come down the aisles and were now pounding on the wooden stage with their fists. Many of them were shouting "Deep River" and "Heaven, Heaven" with their deep Russian voices. Marian sang several encores. "It was disconcerting for a few minutes," she said, "but how could one resist such enthusiasm?"[16]

This was Marian's introduction to the special enthusiasm of the Russian audience, which Kosti described as follows:

> The Russian concert public is probably one of the most sensitive in the world, and it is a real joy to perform for these people. They show their appreciation by hand clapping, vocal outbursts, and stamping their feet; and one feels that their appreciation comes from the depths of their hearts. This enthusiasm was noticeable at the opera, in the theaters, and especially at the performance of a ballet. Russians respond quickly to things artistic.[17]

In Moscow, Marian met Mikhail Ippolitov-Ivanov, the former director of the Moscow Conservatory and the composer of *Caucasian Sketches* and other Russian pieces, who was still active in the Russian musical world. At his apartment where Marian and Kosti were invited to dinner, Marian enjoyed the lively, friendly Russian atmosphere, over which the large, bearded Ippolitov-Ivanov presided like a patriarch. Marian found his unusual way of serving food especially amusing. When he saw that the plate of one of his guests was empty, he unfolded his special fork, which was more than a meter long and, wielding it like a skilled fencer, stabbed a piece of bread or meat pie and served it to the guest. One of the guests, the famous soprano, Antonina Nezhdanova, also took a special interest in Marian and attended her Moscow concerts.

Marian's second tour of the Soviet Union was a year later in the spring of 1936, after she had spent three months back in the United States. On this more extensive tour, she sang in Leningrad, Moscow, Kiev, Kharkov, Rostov, Odessa, Tbilisi, Baku, and Kislovodsk.

Marian gave nine concerts in the great hall of the Moscow Conservatory, and while she was in the Soviet capital, she met many leading Russian artists and musicians. Konstantin Stanislavsky, the director of the Moscow Art Theater, gave a tea in Marian's honor and took a special interest in her. He even wanted her to stay in Moscow to study the operatic role of Carmen under his direction. Marian liked opera and thought about it from time to time. She had even been asked to sing in an opera in Brussels, but the idea never got past the discussion stage.

To study the opera *Carmen* with Stanislavsky was a unique opportunity, but Marian doubted her acting ability, and she knew she was no dancer. Besides, she was committed to her European tour. She hoped someday to return to Moscow to study with the Russian master, but she never did. Stanislavsky died two years later, leaving Marian sorry she had not accepted his offer. "It would have been wise to grasp that opportunity," she said, "even at the expense of postponing the tour."[18]

Marian was later asked if Stalin or any of the other top Communists attended her concerts. She answered not that she knew of, but she wasn't sure. At one of the concerts when there was a lot of excitement backstage, she and Kosti were told that a very important person was going to be in attendance. When the concert began, the crimson curtains of the large center box were drawn. Marian and Kosti assumed that nobody was in the box, but at the intermission they were told that the drawn curtains meant that the box was occupied. Somebody whispered that Stalin was in it. Was he? Marian never found out for sure.

Later in Marian's tour, in Tbilisi, the capital of Georgia, Marian's concert was postponed because the Georgian orchestra she was supposed to sing with was a day late getting back from its tour. When the people who had assembled in the outdoor theater were told the concert had to be postponed, Marian was impressed with the way they quietly filed out and then returned the next night and filled every seat. The night the concert was postponed, Marian and Kosti were taken to hear authentic Georgian music, which they found strange but fascinating.

On the day before Marian's concert in the Azerbaijanian oil city of Baku on the Caspian Sea, Marian and Kosti heard an orchestra of sixty men using instruments neither of them had ever seen before and playing music that was, according to Kosti, "only a rhythmic noise, utterly unenjoyable to European ears."[19] Marian wondered if people whose music was so different from Western music would warm up to her kind of songs, but her worries were laid to rest when the very same people who found the orchestra's exotic music so enjoyable greeted her songs with storms of enthusiastic applause.

Marian and Kosti returned to Tbilisi for a trip to the Russian summer resort of Kislovodsk near the Black Sea. When the Soviet government invited them to rest for a month as its guests, they were only too happy to accept. However, the journey to Kislovodsk proved to be a trip that Marian never forgot. It began on a rainy day when she and Kosti headed out of Tbilisi in a large open truck that contained many other passengers. It crossed the Caucasus Mountains through the Georgian Pass to Vladikavkas, where they were supposed to meet the airplane that was to fly them to Kislovodsk. But the plane never arrived. There were no trains, and after three days of rain, the roads were impassable. So Marian and Kosti had to make their own arrangements through the hotel for a plane.

A young man who said he was their guide drove them out to an open field that showed no signs of being an airport. After a very long wait, a small airplane appeared and landed at the far end of the field. Marian and Kosti and their luggage were driven across the bumpy field in an open horse-drawn cart to the waiting plane. There they helped the pilot load the baggage and got in. The guide sat up front with the pilot; Marian and Kosti were crammed together in the back seat.

They then took off for what turned out to be a flying nightmare. The guide apparently told the pilot to do some stunts for Miss Anderson's amusement, so he did loops and spirals. Only with great difficulty was Kosti finally able to communicate to the pilot that they were not amused. When they landed, Marian felt so wretched that she could barely walk or talk.

Since there was no other transportation for them, they had to make the journey into Kislovodsk once more in a horse-drawn wagon. They set their luggage in the center of the wagon bed so it would not slide off, and they sat on either side of it with their feet dangling over the side. The rocky road shook the wagon so much that Marian felt as if her insides were falling apart.

The guide checked them into the hotel in Kislovodsk, and they all followed the Russian bellboy up to the third floor and down a long hallway. Marian assumed that the three of them would have separate rooms, but when the bellboy opened the door of the corner room, she saw that it contained three beds! Marian said they could not possibly take the room, so Kosti took the guide back downstairs and eventually came back with everything settled. Marian was pleased to find out she had a room of her own, as was her practice, not in the hotel, which was very crowded, but in a comfortable sanatorium not far away.

Marian never got used to certain Russian customs, such as the practice of putting strangers together in sleeping compartments on the trains and in the same hotel rooms. She was also curious about the practice on trains of having tea poured from a samovar into glasses and of buying food at stations when the train stopped.

On her first tour, Marian was fascinated by the Russians who came to her concerts in the bitter cold winter. The audiences, who arrived all bundled up like "monstrous, stuffed creatures," would undergo a transformation in the cloakroom. After shedding their heavy fur-lined overcoats, they took off their heavy boots, which they had stuffed with newspapers, and put on their good shoes, which they had carried separately in paper bags or in the pockets of their coats. By the time they took their seats in the hall, they looked very different from the way they had when they first arrived.

Marian also had a problem with the way the Russians paid her for her concerts. They insisted on paying her with rubles, which they packed tightly and wrapped in old newspapers, making each bundle of rubles feel like a large brick. Since the Russians did not pay Marian after every concert, the rubles they owed her piled up, so that a great many of these bulky bundles would arrive at the same time. After a while, Marian wasn't quite sure what to do with them. They were too bulky and heavy to carry around in her suitcase. As the tour progressed, she even stopped opening the bundles to count the rubles because it took so long and it was so much trouble to rewrap each bundle.

The Soviets did not allow visitors to exchange their rubles for foreign currency or take them out of the country, so Marian had to spend her earnings in the Soviet Union. Even though she bought many things for herself and her friends—

capes, pearls, diamonds, antiques—she had trouble spending her Russian money. People used to follow her around and come to her hotel to try to sell her things.

At the end of the tour in Moscow, Marian and Kosti felt very rich, but they knew that they had to spend all their rubles before they left the Soviet Union. On the day before they left, Kosti went to the park and sat on a bench to enjoy the scenery. He noticed that there were many old, poor people in the park. When a half-starved old woman on crutches hobbled over in his direction, he took out his largest ruble bill and folded it up in his hand. As she passed, he slipped it into her hand.

When she looked at it and saw how much it was, she cried with joy and fell down at Kosti's feet. She kissed his shoes and embraced his feet so tightly that he felt her trembling. Kosti, noticing that people were staring, tried to pull away, but the woman held on. When Kosti saw a policeman approaching and told the woman he was coming, she folded the bill, grabbed her crutches, and disappeared into the bushes.

Marian spent her last day shopping, but she was still left with 5,000 rubles, which she was not allowed to take out of the Soviet Union or convert into any other currency. At the border, she had to deposit her extra money in a Russian bank, which issued her a certificate as proof that the money was on deposit there in her name. However, there it sat unused. Marian never did get a chance to claim it or spend it because she never returned to the Soviet Union.

Marian's tour of Europe made her a success there in a way she never had been in the United States. Yet she never thought seriously about settling in Europe, as some American black artists had done and as many of Marian's European friends advised. She could have asked her mother and sisters to move to Europe so they could all live together as a family, but Marian would not think of it. "Moving the family would have meant uprooting it, and I had no right to place my career ahead of my family's interests." She also thought about her friends and neighbors in Philadelphia who had supported her through the years. "They had not helped me and had faith in me just to see me run away to Europe."

Furthermore, Marian was eager to return home and put herself to the test as an artist in her own country. "I had gone to Europe to achieve something, to reach for a place as a serious artist, but I never doubted that I must return. I was—and am—an American."[20]

Portrait of the young artist, Marian Anderson

*In concert in Moscow in 1935, the American singer
was received by enthusiastic Russian audiences.*

"One of the greatest singers of our time." —N. Y. TIMES

MARIAN ANDERSON

"acclaimed greatest concert singer of today"

"holds audience in spell"

"sings way into city's heart"

"leaves lasting impression"

"hailed by huge audience at thrilling concert"

"wild ovation attests to singer's artistry"

"scores brilliant triumph"

—HEADLINES IN AMERICA'S PRESS

The famous Lincoln Memorial Easter concert in April 1939. After being refused the right to perform at Constitution Hall in Washington, D.C., Miss Anderson sang outdoors to approximately 75,000 people.

*Miss Anderson received the prestigious Philadelphia Bok Award,
presented annually to the person of whom the city was most proud.
She was the first black in the city's history to receive this award.*

Opposite: *Eleanor Roosevelt presenting the Spingarn Medal to
Marian Anderson in 1939. This was an award presented to
an American black who had achieved the most during the year.*

*The American singer always spent a great deal of time
and care going over her musical programs before a concert.
She is joined here by her accompanist, Franz Rupp.*

Opposite: *The singer and her husband,
Orpheus "King" Fisher*

Backed by the voices of U.S. troops, the famed concert singer leads the way with a song somewhere near the front lines in Korea in 1957.

Opposite: *A triumphant Marian Anderson in her debut at the Metropolitan Opera in New York City as Ulrica, the sorceress in Verdi's* A Masked Ball

In the conference room of the General Assembly of the
United Nations, where Miss Anderson served as U.S.
delegate by appointment of President Dwight Eisenhower

In her role as one of the founders of the U.S. Freedom from Hunger Foundation, Miss Anderson is introduced by President John F. Kennedy to German Chancellor Konrad Adenauer. From left to right: Marian Anderson, George McGovern, President Kennedy, Adenauer, and Mrs. Woodrow Wilson.

Being congratulated at the White House by President
Lyndon B. Johnson during presentation ceremonies of the
Presidential Medal of Freedom, the highest award an American
president can give to a citizen during peacetime.

Opposite: *Arms laden with flowers, the concert
singer leaves the stage of Carnegie Hall after her
farewell concert on April 19, 1965.*

First lady Rosalynn Carter chats with Miss Anderson at the benefit concert celebrating the singer's seventy-fifth birthday.

Sopranos Shirley Verrett (l) and Grace Bumbry (r) on hand for the famed singer's eightieth birthday salute. Being the first black soloist to appear at the Metropolitan Opera, Marian Anderson paved the way for other black artists.

CHAPTER 4

Back Home

While Marian was making her highly successful tour through the cities of Europe in 1935, she received a cable from Sol Hurok informing her that her first American concert was going to be on December 30 in New York's Town Hall, the very same auditorium that had been the scene of her greatest disappointment years before. Marian felt a sudden pang, but the moment passed quickly. She had learned so much since then. She had studied with the finest teachers, sung in the best halls, and received applause and praise from the leading figures in the world of music. This time she knew she was ready.

Right away Marian was faced with a difficult decision. Who should be her accompanist in the United States—Kosti or Billy? Kosti Vehanen had accompanied her all over Europe and had taught her so much. He was a master musician in his own right and had helped her develop her repertory of songs in many different languages. Yet Billy King was her old friend who had helped her get started and had been with her through all the lean years.

Marian knew Billy would understand if she chose Kosti, but she thought other blacks might feel offended. They might wonder why she had chosen a European white man over someone of her own race. Why should a black musician work hard to become a good accompanist if there were not going to be any openings for him? Also, if Marian chose Kosti, there could be trouble in the South, where some people might take offense at a black singer appearing on the same stage with a white accompanist.

Kosti was eager for the assignment and disturbed that he might not get it. He told Marian, "If I can come and play only the first pieces on the program, I will charm them so that they will want me to stay." In the end, Marian made the decision on strictly musical grounds. She chose Kosti to be her accompanist.

Town Hall Concert

Marian started preparing for her Town Hall concert in September while she was still touring Europe. She and Kosti spent every free moment working on her repertory. Kosti believed in planning the order of the songs for maximum effect, putting the *Schlagers* (knockouts) at the close of each group where they would have the greatest impact. By the time Marian and Kosti finished touring Europe and sailed for America on December 17, they had prepared the Town Hall program and had decided on the order of the songs. On board the beautiful *Ile de France* on Marian's sixth voyage across the Atlantic, they practiced every day in a room with a piano, which the purser let them use.

One day Marian was relaxing on a deck chair under a warm blanket and watching the waves of the rough sea when she noticed that it was time to meet Kosti for rehearsal. She got up and went to the nearest staircase, but just as she put her hand on the railing, the ship lurched, causing Marian to lose her grip and tumble down the steps. As she lay at the bottom of the stairs, her first thought was: Will I be able to give the concert? When she got up and put weight on her left foot, a sharp pain shot through her ankle, forcing her to hobble along the passageway to the rehearsal room.

Kosti could see that she was in pain. She told him about her fall but insisted she was all right. Nevertheless, Kosti sent for the ship's doctor. There was no X-ray machine on board, so the doctor could not tell if her ankle was broken, but he told her that she must stay off it.

For the next two days Marian lay in her cabin to keep weight off her swollen ankle. She had promised the captain that she would sing at the ship's benefit concert, and she was determined to keep her promise. On the night of the concert, wearing a long dress that covered her bandaged ankle, she was put in a wheelchair and wheeled down a back passageway to the door of the salon. Since she did not want anyone to see the wheelchair or make a fuss about her accident, she walked the short distance from the door to the piano by herself and sang for the ship's passengers. Then she returned to her cabin, where she stayed for the rest of the trip.

When the ship arrived in New York, the doctor wanted Marian wheeled down the gangplank, but Marian did not want to alarm her family and friends who were waiting for her. Instead, she had the bandages removed, got into her most comfortable sports shoes, and limped down the gangplank as best she could. By the time Marian got through customs and met her family and friends, she was too excited to think about her ankle. The excitement continued that night back home in Philadelphia as relatives, neighbors, and friends from the church crowded around her. With all the fuss, she did not have time to worry about her ankle.

The next morning when Marian looked at her ankle, she was disturbed at what she saw. The swelling was down, but her entire foot felt numb and her toes were a bluish green. Marian's sister took her to the hospital where an X-ray revealed that Marian had a fractured ankle. The doctor put her foot in a cast that covered everything from her toes to her knee and told her that the cast would have to stay on for six weeks. Marian was given a pair of crutches to help her get around while she was in the cast.

With the Town Hall concert only a week away, Marian felt desperate. Some friends urged her to postpone the concert, but how could she do that? This New York concert, coming after her long sojourn in Europe, was the most important concert of her life. Mr. Hurok had publicized the concert with ads, posters, programs, and invitations to New York's leading critics and the most important opinion makers in the world of music.

Although her cast was large and cumbersome and she needed the crutches to get around, Marian was not in great pain. She knew she could manage if she set her mind to it. There was nothing else to do but sing and make the best of it.

Mr. Hurok wanted Marian to stay in a midtown hotel close to Town Hall rather than at the YWCA in Harlem, but when he tried to make a reservation, none of the hotels would accept her. Marian Anderson, who had been acclaimed and honored all across Europe, was not welcome at a single hotel in midtown Manhattan because she was black. Refusing to be upset, Marian told Sol Hurok that the Harlem YWCA would be perfectly fine, and that was where she stayed. Marian's upper leg and toes needed to be massaged regularly in order to keep her circulation moving, so the doctor made sure a nurse accompanied Marian to New York.

The day before the concert, there was a press conference in Mr. Hurok's office. Marian sat behind a desk so that the reporters would not see her cast. She wanted to be judged for her voice alone—not on the basis of her color or her accident. She certainly was not interested in getting sympathy for her injury.

On December 30, 1935, Marian left the Harlem YWCA on her crutches and took the long taxi ride south to Town Hall. When she arrived, there was much discussion about the best way to get Marian on and off the stage. Usually at a recital, the curtains are open while the audience enters the hall and the singer and accompanist come on stage. However, this time the curtains were left closed while the audience came in and took their seats. Then, when it was time to begin, the lights dimmed and the curtains opened.

Kosti and the nurse had already helped Marian onto the stage, so that when the curtains opened Marian was standing at the bend of the piano, looking resplendent in her black and gold brocade gown, which fell to the floor over the hidden cast. Putting weight on her foot without the help of the crutches caused her some pain, but it was not intense enough to be a real problem.

The audience applauded warmly, completely unaware that anything was amiss. Marian refused to allow any opening announcement to the audience about her problem. To tell the audience that she was singing with a fractured ankle was to invite pity, and pity was the last thing she wanted. "I was there to present myself as an artist and to be judged by that standard only."[1]

Leaning slightly on the piano, Marian smiled and then nodded to Kosti that she was ready. Closing her eyes and blocking out everything else but her music, she began singing Handel's "Begrüssung," a work so difficult that it is rarely sung in concert. Opening with a long, sustained tone that begins softly and builds slowly to a crescendo, it is a challenge of the highest order for a singer. Marian had sung it in Europe quite successfully, but this was a crucial test, since she was opening her program with it. Mr. Hurok had advised against starting with such a difficult piece, but Marian wanted to strive for the highest level of achievement.

The audience seemed to be on Marian's side even before she opened her mouth. Just knowing that her mother, sisters, and friends, including Mr. Boghetti and King Fisher, were there gave Marian confidence as she sang the difficult Handel piece. By the end of the song, she knew the audience was completely with her. The responsiveness of the audience continued to lift her spirits and make her forget her ankle, as she sang groups of songs by Handel, Schubert, and Sibelius, a Verdi aria, and a final group of spirituals. Marian felt that her voice could have been better in certain places, but she was glad she had been able to stay completely focused on her singing, despite her broken ankle and the heavy cast.

Marian did not allow the audience to be informed about

her injury until after the intermission. She knew that by then she had been judged on the merits of her singing. Marian thought it would be better to tell the audience herself rather than have them read about her ankle in the papers the next morning. (News about her accident had already gotten out to some of the reporters.) When Marian told the audience about her ankle after the intermission, the house burst into sustained applause in tribute to her courage.

By the time Marian came to "The Crucifixion" and the spirituals that she had sung since she was a little girl and thought of as songs with a special spiritual message, she sang them with intense conviction. "When I reached them I felt as if I had come home, fully and unreservedly—not only because they were the songs I had sung from childhood but also because the program was almost finished, and I had survived."

After the curtain fell on her last song, Marian felt both relieved and weary. She had done her best, and the most important concert in her career was now over. People flocked backstage to congratulate and praise her, and the reviews in the papers the next morning were enthusiastic. Howard Taubman of *The New York Times* hailed Marian's homecoming concert as follows:

> Let it be said at the outset: Marian Anderson has returned to her native land one of the great singers of our time. The Negro contralto who has been abroad for four years established herself in her concert at the Town Hall last night as the possessor of an excelling voice and art. Her singing enchanted an audience that included singers. There was no doubt of it, she was mistress of all she surveyed.[2]

The Harlem Y was flooded with calls for Marian from reporters wanting interviews and society people wanting to give parties for her, but Marian was not one to bask in her glory. The day after the concert, she took the train back home to Philadelphia. Although she felt good about her New York performance, she was under no illusions that her struggle was over. "I knew that this was not the end of the quest to be an artist. It was, I felt, a beginning—a new beginning."[3]

After all the excitement died down, Marian went back over all the music she had sung at Town Hall, song by song and note by note, to see where she might have sung more softly or more deeply or more powerfully. *Time* magazine was impressed that Marian chose to go home to Philadelphia rather than capitalize on her sure-fire success. "She could have been roundly feted if she had chosen to remain in Manhattan," the article said. "Instead, she preferred to hide away in her mother's Philadelphia home, with its starched lace curtains, its overstuffed furniture, its radio, its fireplace aglow with artificial flames."[4]

Under Sol Hurok's Management

Sol Hurok had planned Marian's first concert tour with great care, aiming initially for fifteen concerts. In the wake of the excitement created by Marian's Town Hall appearance, however, he quickly arranged a concert at Carnegie Hall, which was immediately sold out. There, and in the other halls where she performed with her cast still on, the stage curtains were kept closed and opened only when Marian and Kosti were in their places. If the hall did not have curtains, Marian hobbled on stage as best she could. Although everybody knew about the accident and was understanding, Marian felt awkward about the arrangement and counted the days until the removal of the cast.

Mr. Hurok had not lined up the fifteen concerts he had hoped to, but he had reason to feel satisfied with Marian's return to the United States, thanks in large part to her successes at Town Hall and Carnegie Hall. Many people had warned him that he would have trouble promoting Marian Anderson in the United States because racial prejudice was just too strong. Someone high up in the concert business told him bluntly, "You won't be able to give her away." Others thought that sending her out with a white accompanist might cause an additional problem. One of Mr. Hurok's associates told him that New York was one thing, but "in other cities she might be stoned." No such thing happened. All in all, Mr. Hurok had reason to feel good about Marian's first American tour. "Marian sang," he said, "and her audiences fell at her feet."

From the start, Marian appreciated Mr. Hurok's sensitivity and good taste and liked the dignified way he handled the publicity and scheduling of her concerts. He could have booked more concerts, but instead he chose the engagements very carefully, not caring if he took a loss the first season. The normal practice in the music world was for the performer to pay for the New York concert, as Marian had done for her first Town Hall appearance, but Mr. Hurok chose to absorb the costs of Marian's New York recitals at both Town Hall and Carnegie Hall.

Marian appreciated Mr. Hurok's deep personal interest in her career. She knew he wanted every concert in America to be right, and he refused to accept any that were not. Nor did he complain, as some managers might have done, about Marian going back to Europe, even though returning to Europe might mean passing up invitations for American concerts.

For Marian, Sol Hurok was more than just a manager. He was an impresario of great imagination who was willing to take chances when he believed in an artist or ensemble. Over the years that they worked together, Marian and Mr. Hurok developed a strong friendship and artistic partnership that were important for Marian's career.

They came to have the highest respect for each other. Mr. Hurok never met anyone who had the strength of character and dignity Marian had. "I have seen her in all sorts of awesome situations," he said. "I have seen her tremulous, even moved to tears by the honors that have come to her. But I have never seen her flustered. There is about Marian a poise even under the stress of great emotion, a dignity and a beauty of speech and manner that are unshakable because they come from within."[5]

For her part, Marian credited Mr. Hurok with making her career a success. "I owe more than I can say to this fabulous man," she said. Then she added with characteristic modesty, "There must be other performers who were better equipped for a great career and who were simply not lucky enough to have Mr. Hurok at the helm."[6]

Europe and South America

After Marian's first American tour under the Hurok management, she returned to Europe in the spring of 1936 for another long, successful tour. After a concert in Queen's Hall in London, Marian went to Paris where she sang at the world-famous opera house. Only the Russian pianist and composer, Sergei Rachmaninoff, and the Austrian violinist, Fritz Kreisler, had ever sold out the Paris Opera for a solo performance, but Marian did just that with her debut there.

Kosti had always encouraged Marian to dress elegantly for her concerts and had accompanied soloists a number of times at the glittering opera house, but even he was dazzled that night by Marian's stunning gown of gold lamé with long, tight sleeves. The dress had been made especially for Marian's debut. "When she appeared in this brilliant gown, with the diamond brooch and the topaz ring, in the golden surroundings of l'Opéra, no one could believe that this statuesque woman was the same young girl who, four years previously, had cut the little train off her gown as she said, 'That's too much.' "[7]

Marian sang in Holland and Belgium and then returned to the scenes of her successes in Austria the summer before.

In Vienna she sang the Brahms "Rhapsody" with the famous conductor Bruno Walter and then performed two concerts at the Salzburg Music Festival.

After appearing in Budapest, The Hague, and other cities, Marian enjoyed a short vacation on the Riviera in the south of France, where she rented a villa between Nice and Monte Carlo. While she loved the sunny days and the blue Mediterranean, she spent most of her time studying French songs with the noted vocal teacher, Germaine de Castro, in a music studio on the ground floor of the villa. Marian and her teacher worked an average of three sessions a day, so that by the end of Marian's "vacation," she could sing songs as flawlessly in French as in German.

Marian then gave concerts in Barcelona, Valencia, and Bilbao in Spain, where the civil war that was to tear the country apart for the next three years had already begun. Everywhere Marian and Kosti went they heard talk of war, and they finally had to cut short their tour because of it. "As we came over the border into France," Kosti wrote, "we both looked sadly back, thinking of poor, beautiful Spain and the terrible future she was facing."[8]

From Europe, Marian and Kosti traveled to South America. Boarding the liner *Augustus* in Cannes on the French Riviera, they sailed through the Straits of Gibraltar into the Atlantic and then down the African coast. Marian had always dreamed of seeing her ancestral Africa someday, so she was naturally excited when they approached Dakar, the capital of Senegal, for a brief stopover. "Marian seemed happy as her feet touched African soil," said Kosti. "I think for her it was like coming home, actually to be in the land where her forefathers had lived for hundreds of years."[9]

On their walk from the pier into the center of the city, Marian watched with great curiosity the native women, dressed in colorful robes and wearing elegant coiffures. The women stared back with equal interest. As she and Kosti drove around the city in a taxi, Marian was fascinated by the noble faces and regal bearing of the people who were so different and yet so similar.

From Dakar, the ship sailed across the Atlantic to Brazil, where Marian performed in Rio de Janeiro and São Paulo. One day they drove to a large snake farm outside São Paulo. After they had walked through the farm, they found themselves alone at the edge of a large pit that contained giant poisonous frogs and the farm's biggest snakes.

While Marian was taking pictures, one of the largest snakes tried to escape. After trying several times to reach the top of the wall, the snake finally got enough of its upper part over the wall to swing the rest of its body up and over. For a moment, the snake lay still. Marian went up to it and snapped more pictures. Kosti observed, "She did not seem to be in the least afraid."[10]

As the snake made its way toward the road, Kosti ran for the caretaker. When they returned, Marian was following the snake, still snapping pictures. The caretaker grabbed the snake by the neck and shouted, *"Não liberdade!"* ("No freedom for you"). Then he took it back to the pit. Kosti found out from a friend who visited the snake farm the next year that the caretaker enjoyed telling tourists how his biggest snake got loose the day Marian Anderson visited the farm.

In Buenos Aires, Argentina, Marian gave twelve concerts in seven weeks. Despite the fact that Lily Pons and other well-known singers were in the city at the same time, Marian's concerts were well attended and highly praised. She was also very well received in Montevideo, Uruguay. Clearly, Marian seemed as able to touch people in South America through the international language of music as in Europe.

Singing in America

Marian knew that the real test awaited her in the United States. She had conquered Europe, impressed South America, and won applause in New York, but what about the rest of the United States? What about the South, where prejudice against blacks was deeply rooted?

By the time Marian returned from Europe and South America, Mr. Hurok had scheduled a long, intensive tour of over a hundred concerts in more than seventy American cities. Perhaps this tour would answer some basic questions about Marian's future as an artist in the United States. Would she be accepted in her own country, which had yet to come to terms with its own race problem? Would she be welcome in the South? How would audiences react to her appearance on stage with a white accompanist? Would black people be allowed to attend her concerts on a fair and equal basis?

Marian's first extensive American tour in 1937 took her to the finest concert halls in the country. In the South, just her appearance on the stages of these halls made history. The southern audiences who came to hear her were, for the most part, intelligent and fair-minded. At first, her appearance with Kosti was something of a shock, but soon the magic of Marian's voice caused people to forget race and lose themselves in her singing. The vigorous applause at her concerts was a tribute both to Marian's singing and to her courage.

Southern newspapers reviewed her concerts, and that, too, was a breakthrough. While they praised her singing, however, they were careful not to offend their readers by addressing her as "Miss Anderson," since titles of respect were reserved for white people. Instead, the papers called her "Singer Anderson" or simply "Marian Anderson." However, the papers did break a southern taboo by describing her as beautiful and by praising her clothes.

When Marian appeared in segregated southern halls where blacks were seated in a separate section, usually in the balcony, she always bowed first to her own people, then to the rest of the audience. This was her way of letting people know that she was proud of being black.

Over the years, Marian changed the way blacks were

seated at her concerts. The general practice had been to have blacks seated in the worst locations in the hall, but Marian insisted that the black sections be located in the better parts of the hall. As Marian became better known, her audiences became increasingly white, so she also insisted that blacks be allowed to buy their seats on a first-come, first-served basis, rather than only being able to buy the tickets that were left over after the whites bought theirs. Finally, when Marian became famous, she insisted that blacks and whites sit together at her concerts. She refused to sing in any hall that had segregated seating.

Marian's long American tour was so successful and she was so popular with lovers of good music that the Hurok office was swamped with requests. People wrote and called for Marian to perform concerts, sing on the radio, and make records. The problem for the Hurok office was no longer getting engagements for Marian, but deciding which ones to accept.

The Hurok people tried to protect Marian from the prejudice they encountered when they sought to book her into hotels closer to concert halls but generally closed to blacks. But Marian ran into enough prejudice anyway. Sometimes to avoid offending white guests, hotel managers suggested that she eat her meals in her room rather than in the dining room. Then there were hundreds of little looks and slights along the way, which Marian tried to ignore, swallowing the hurt as best she could. She believed strongly that music had the power to melt the walls that separated people and that singing was her best weapon against prejudice. Marian once said that drops of water wear away a stone. By maintaining her dignity and pride wherever she went, she won many people over.

Marian ran into prejudice in the North as well as in the South. Once when she went to Springfield, Illinois, to sing at the opening of the film *Young Mr. Lincoln*, she was refused a room in the city's main hotel. Another time she was presented with the keys to Atlantic City, but she was not allowed to stay there overnight. Many restaurants refused to serve Marian and Kosti, and some people even refused to shake Marian's hand. Marian had a certain sympathy for prejudiced people, believing they were motivated more by fear and ignorance than by malice. She refused to let people's limitations distract her from her first priority—her commitment to music.

Kosti remained Marian's accompanist until 1940 and played the piano for her in over 150 American cities, but he confessed that he understood race problems less and less the longer he stayed in the country. "I still have to understand why the worth of a person seems to depend on the color of the skin," he wrote in 1941.

By the time Kosti returned to Finland, he had the highest respect for Marian, believing "that a person with her magnificent calmness and her deep understanding and fine character can through her great art help to wipe away many differences of opinion among the various races." His conclusion was that "every race ought to be very grateful that a human being such as Miss Anderson is giving her message of peace to a world filled with hatred and misunderstanding."[11]

In his memoirs, published in 1946, Sol Hurok discussed Marian's approach to the race issue:

> The Negro people can thank what Providence watches over the oppressed that it was given to them to offer Marian to the world. She is no militant fighter. She makes no complaint, creates no issues, offers no angry protest at the indignities that have been visited upon her because of her color. . . . She has been herself, strong in her inner integrity. And by being herself she has won citadels that have never been breached by doughtier warriors.[12]

In 1936, one of the citadels that Marian won was the White House. President Franklin D. Roosevelt and Mrs.

Roosevelt invited Marian to give a private recital after a small dinner. Marian was delighted when Mrs. Roosevelt thought to invite Marian's mother. When Marian was ushered into the music room on the second floor of the White House, President Roosevelt, who was sitting on a large sofa next to a roaring fire, greeted her. "Why, hello there, Miss Anderson," he said, shaking her hand warmly, "you look just like your photographs, don't you?"

Marian was so speechless that she never did give the little speech she had prepared, but President Roosevelt quickly put her at ease with his friendly manner. According to Kosti, Marian "sang with a special fire and power." When she finished, she was touched by what Mrs. Roosevelt did next. The First Lady took Marian's mother by the hand and led her across the room to introduce her to the president.

Easter Concert

In 1938, Howard University in Washington requested a Marian Anderson concert from the Hurok office. Mr. Hurok set a date—April 9, 1939—and requested a reservation at Constitution Hall, the foremost and largest concert hall in the nation's capital. Marian had sung in Washington before, but only at schools and churches.

When the Hurok office sought to rent Constitution Hall on that date, they were told that that date was taken. When Mr. Hurok suggested other dates, he was informed that all those dates were taken, too. The hall was owned by the Daughters of the American Revolution (D.A.R.), members of which were descendants of the men who had fought against the British in the American Revolution. It soon came out that the D.A.R. had a clause in its lease that prohibited blacks from performing at the hall.

When the news got out that the D.A.R. had refused to rent Constitution Hall for a Marian Anderson concert, the world was shocked. Public officials, religious leaders, writers, and private citizens from different walks of life protested. Leading musicians canceled their concerts at Constitution Hall. One such musician was the famous violinist, Jascha Heifetz, who said he would now be ashamed to play there. Hundreds of other people from the music world sent telegrams and letters of protest. One critic spoke for many when he wired the D.A.R. that their action subverted the U.S. Constitution and put the D.A.R. on the side of those who sought to destroy democracy.

The most dramatic protest came from Eleanor Roosevelt, who was herself a member of the D.A.R. In her nationally syndicated newspaper column, "My Day," she announced her resignation from the D.A.R., an action that made headlines in newspapers all across the country. Marian, who had sensed while touring the West that something was amiss with regard to the negotiations for renting the hall, did not find out about what was going on until she reached San Francisco. On her way to a performance there she passed a newsstand and saw the headline: "Mrs. Roosevelt Takes Stand—Resigns From D.A.R." When Marian read about the controversy after her concert, she was amazed that things had gone so far. She was also impressed by Eleanor Roosevelt. "What a wonderful woman she is!" she told Kosti. "She not only knows what is right, but she also does the right thing."[13]

Other members of the D.A.R. and even some local chapters protested the action of their national body in Washington. Marian said that their protests "confirmed my conviction that a whole group should not be condemned because an individual or section of the group does a thing that is not right."[14] There were voices on the other side, too, like the columnist who thought the whole affair was a publicity stunt on behalf of a "hitherto obscure Negro singer."

Howard University, which still wanted the concert, asked the Board of Education of Washington, D.C., for permission to use the large auditorium of Central High School, but the request was turned down. Thousands of people protested the board's decision by signing petitions and picketing the office. An editorial in the Central High student newspaper came out strongly in favor of hosting "one of the musical world's greatest artists."

In the meantime, as the controversy continued and Marian made her way back across the country on her tour, reporters asked her questions at every stop. Reluctant to get involved in the controversy, Marian said little. She told the reporters only that she trusted the Hurok office to handle the problem in the best possible way and that she believed a way would be found for her to sing in Washington.

When Kosti became seriously ill in St. Louis, he had to be sent back to Washington to be hospitalized. To take his place as Marian's accompanist, the Hurok office sent out Franz Rupp, an experienced pianist whom Marian had never met. When they went over the program of her upcoming concert, Marian was impressed with the way Franz could transpose a song into a different key at sight and could play from memory many of the songs she was going to sing.

Marian gave her concert in St. Louis and sang two more recitals on her way back east. The first thing she wanted to do when she got to Washington was to visit Kosti in the hospital, but she knew that the controversy would be waiting for her when she arrived. Gerald Goode, head of public relations for the Hurok office, met her in Annapolis and used the train ride to the capital to fill Marian in on what to expect.

At the train station, Marian was surrounded by an army of newspaper reporters who fired questions at her. She could not answer most of them because she did not have enough information about the fine points of the negotiations that were going on. Anyway, she just wanted to escape the press and go to visit Kosti. She finally got to the waiting car and was driven off, but the reporters followed her to the hospital and waited for her to come out.

The furor over the Washington concert followed Marian everywhere she went as she fulfilled her other concert dates in the East before Easter. Photographers and reporters were everywhere, and all sorts of people, friends and strangers alike, approached her to discuss the issue and express their sympathy and support.

Finally, Mr. Hurok made an announcement that Marian was going to sing in Washington after all, but not in Constitution Hall. At the invitation of the Department of the Interior of the U.S. government, Marian was going to sing an outdoor concert at the Lincoln Memorial on Easter Sunday.

From the beginning, Marian had felt more sorrow than anger over the affair, saying, "The unpleasantness disturbed me, and if it had been up to me alone I would have sought a way to wipe it out." She was the first to admit that she was not temperamentally suited to controversy and strife: "I have been in this world long enough to know that there are all kinds of people, all suited by their own natures for different tasks. It would be fooling myself to think that I was meant to be a fearless fighter; I was not, just as I was not meant to be a soprano instead of a contralto." Marian had reservations about the concert at the Lincoln Memorial, but she consented. "I said yes, but the yes did not come easily or quickly."

In fact, Marian had her own private doubts about the concert right up to the time she gave it. "In principle the idea was sound, but it could not be comfortable to me as an individual. As I thought further, I could see that my significance as an individual was small in this affair. I had become, whether I liked it or not, a symbol representing my people. I had to appear."

On Easter morning Mr. Hurok met Marian and her family at the train station and drove them to the home of Gifford Pinchot, the former governor of Pennsylvania, where they stayed until it was time for the concert. Kosti, who was well again, joined them. At the appointed time, Marian and her party were escorted to the Lincoln Memorial by police on motorcycles. Because there were rumors of possible trouble and anxiety about Marian's personal safety, there was a feeling of anticipation in the air that was almost electric.

When the car pulled up behind the Lincoln Memorial and Marian heard the excited murmur of the crowd, a powerful feeling swept over her. "The only comparable emotion I could recall was the feeling I had when Maestro Toscanini had appeared in the artist's room in Salzburg. My heart leaped wildly, and I could not talk. I even wondered whether I would be able to sing."[15]

Whatever she felt inside, Marian maintained her dignified calm, the characteristic that so impressed Sol Hurok and everybody else who knew her. Marian and her party walked through the crowd down the roped-off path to the monument. Mr. Hurok, who was walking beside Marian, said that "the arm which I took to steady her was steadier than my own." As they entered the passageway into the monument, Marian and Kosti were led off into a small waiting room while Marian's family and Mr. Hurok took the seats that had been reserved for them on the platform. Secretary of the Interior Harold Ickes came back to the waiting room to introduce himself and outline the program. Then came the signal to begin.

Marian and Kosti followed Secretary Ickes toward the platform, but waited in the entrance as he stepped forward to the microphones at the center of the platform. The day had begun cloudy and gray, but now the sun was shining. Those with special invitations were seated on the platform—Supreme Court Justice Hugo Black, Secretary of the Treasury Henry Morgenthau, and at least a dozen members of Congress, including Representative Arthur W. Mitchell, a black congressman from Illinois.

Secretary Ickes began his speech by telling the vast audience that under the blue skies all people are free and that "when God gave us this wonderful outdoors and the sun, the moon and the stars, He made no distinction of race or creed or color." Pointing to the monuments of the great presidents that surrounded them, Secretary Ickes mentioned those "even in this great capital of our great democratic Republic, who are either too timid or too indifferent to lift up the light that Jefferson and Lincoln carried aloft."

The secretary of the interior continued: "Genius, like justice, is blind. For genius has touched with the tip of her wing this woman who, if it had not been for the great mind of Lincoln, would not be able to stand among us today as a free individual in a free land. Genius draws no color line. She has endowed Marian Anderson with such a voice as lifts any individual above his fellows, as is a matter of exultant pride to any race. And so it is fitting that Marian Anderson should raise her voice in tribute to the noble Lincoln, whom mankind will ever honor."[16]

Then, turning to Marian, who was waiting in the entrance, he said, "We are grateful to Miss Marian Anderson for coming here to sing for us today." Marian walked slowly between the marble columns toward the center of the monument and stopped in front of the great sculptured figure of Abraham Lincoln. Wearing a black velvet dress, with a mink coat around her shoulders, she looked regal and dignified.

At that moment, Marian paused to look out over the crowd of 75,000 people—men, women, and children, black and white—who were looking up at her as one. "There seemed to be people as far as the eye could see," she said. "The crowd stretched in a great semicircle from the Lincoln Memorial around the reflecting pool on to the shaft of the Washington Monument. I had a feeling that a great wave of goodwill poured out from these people, almost engulfing me."[17] As Marian walked down the steps to the microphones, a thunderous wave of applause swept up over her. For Kosti, it was one of the most moving experiences of his life. "No one who saw her walking that day down the marble steps will ever forget this unusual and wonderful sight," he said, "and few can recall it without tears springing to their eyes."[18]

As the first notes Kosti played were amplified by the

powerful loudspeakers, making the piano sound like ten organs, Marian began singing the national anthem. She was so filled with emotion that, as she later said, "I felt for a moment as though I were choking. For a desperate second I thought that the words, well as I knew them, would not come."[19]

But the words came and sing she did. After the national anthem, Marian sang "America," the aria "O Mio Fernando," Schubert's "Ave Maria," and three spirituals— "Gospel Train," "Trampin'," and "My Soul Is Anchored in the Lord." Not only was this one of the most important concerts in American history, but it was a special, magical occasion as well. Kosti summarized its significance as follows:

> If human beings in their narrow wisdom closed the door of their small halls, then God in His great wisdom opened the door to His most beautiful cathedral, which was decorated that day as for a festival, with lovely green grass, cherry trees in blossom, the large pool mirroring the blue sky, and light clouds leisurely floating by, a soft wind caressing everyone, colored and white—every human being, rich and poor, the strong and the weak, the good and the bad sharing in the beauties so freely bestowed upon them that glorious Easter Sunday.[20]

After Marian finished singing, with the imposing statue of Abraham Lincoln looming up behind her, the applause and cheering of the crowd swelled to a crescendo that would not die down. Marian had not planned to say anything, but she did. She told the crowd: "I am overwhelmed. I just can't talk. I can't tell you what you have done for me today. I thank you from the bottom of my heart again and again."[21]

Aftermath

That epic Easter concert and the name of Marian Anderson were forever linked in the minds and memories of millions of Americans. For years afterward, people came backstage or went up to Marian wherever she was to tell her they had been at the concert or had heard it on the radio. Even when Marian was abroad, people told her how much that Easter Sunday had meant to them.

In June 1939, several weeks after the Easter Sunday concert, Marian was invited to the White House for the second time. She was one of several artists who were invited to perform for the visiting King George VI and Queen Elizabeth of England. This time Marian and Kosti were taken first to the president's private room and then to the room where the other artists—Kate Smith, Lawrence Tibbett of the Metropolitan Opera, and the cowboy singer, Alan Lomax—were waiting for their turn to perform.

When Marian appeared before the royal couple and the other guests, her singing of "Ave Maria" made a deep impression and drew fervent applause. After the artists had all taken their turns, they were presented to the king and queen. Marian had practiced her curtsy, but when she performed it for the queen, whom Kosti described as "a real fairy-tale princess,"[22] it came out badly. Marian began the curtsy looking straight into the queen's eyes, but by the time she finished, she was facing off in another direction. "I don't know how I managed it so inelegantly," she said, "but I never tried one again, not even for the king."

Marian and Eleanor Roosevelt met several times after that—in New York, Hyde Park, Tokyo, and Tel Aviv—since both were among America's most traveled women. Once in Tokyo, when Eleanor Roosevelt found out that Marian Anderson was singing there, she changed her schedule so she could attend Marian's concert. Marian, who called Mrs. Roosevelt "one of the most admirable human beings I have ever met," respected her for the way she was willing to travel for what she believed in at a moment's notice. "I suspect that she has done a great deal for people that has never been divulged publicly," Marian said. "I know what she did for me."[23]

A month after Marian's second White House visit, Mrs.

Roosevelt presented Marian with the Spingarn Medal on behalf of the National Association for the Advancement of Colored People (NAACP). The medal was awarded to the American black who had achieved the most during the year. The citation read:

> Marian Anderson has been chosen for her special achievement in the field of music. Equally with that achievement, which has won her worldwide fame as one of the greatest singers of our time, is her magnificent dignity as a human being. Her unassuming manner, which has not been changed by her phenomenal success, has added to the esteem not only of Marian Anderson as an individual, but of the race to which she belongs.

Marian received another prestigious award in March 1941. Philadelphia honored her with the Bok Award, which the city gave annually to the citizen of whom it was most proud. Marian, who was the first black in the city's history to receive the award, used the $10,000 prize to establish a scholarship fund to help music students of all races. When the original $10,000 ran out, she endowed the fund with her own money. For thirty years, from 1942 to 1972, the Marian Anderson Scholarship Fund helped more than fifty young musicians of all races with scholarships amounting to over $50,000.

During World War II, Marian sang many benefits and special concerts in hospitals and camps for the armed forces. At a shipyard in California, she christened the *Booker T. Washington*, a ship named for the well-known black educator and founder of the Tuskegee Institute. Then she sang for the workers, who cheered her every song and demanded encore after encore. Marian also sang at a special war bond concert in Carnegie Hall, which resulted in the sale of $1,679,000 worth of bonds for the war effort.

In 1943, a large and powerful mural that commemorated the concert for future generations was painted on the wall of the Department of the Interior in Washington. At the unveiling ceremony, which Marian attended, Secretary Ickes said that Marian Anderson's voice and personality had come to symbolize the immortal truth that all men are created free and equal.

In front of reporters and photographers, Marian said that she was deeply touched to be a symbol of democracy and that everyone present at the concert had been "a living witness to the ideals of freedom for which President Lincoln died." Marian concluded by saying, "When I sang that day, I was singing to the entire nation."[24]

On the night after the unveiling of the Easter concert mural at the Department of the Interior, Marian sang in Constitution Hall, the very hall that had excluded her four years earlier. She had sung there twice since 1939, after the anti-black clause was struck out of the rental agreement, but this time the D.A.R. invited her to sing at a benefit for China Relief. After that, Marian sang regularly in Constitution Hall, which was now open to blacks. Her concerts were always sold out. "There was no sense of triumph," she said about finally singing in Constitution Hall. "I felt it was a beautiful concert hall, and I was happy to sing in it."[25]

Throughout Marian's career, she sang benefits for various charities and causes. As a "baby contralto," she had sung with her aunt to help raise money for the building of a church, and she always continued to sing for worthy causes. When Italy invaded Ethiopia in 1936, Marian sang a benefit for the Ethiopian Red Cross in the Royal Opera House in Stockholm. She later sang a benefit recital at the Brooklyn Academy of Music for Finnish war relief in May 1940. Finland had been attacked by the Soviet Union, so Kosti was especially grateful to Marian for helping his people.

Surely the most memorable charity concert—it was certainly the one Kosti remembered best—was the one Marian sang at a maximum security prison in Denmark. The prison, for men serving life sentences, was a complex of large, dark, gloomy buildings situated outside a small Danish city. To reach the warden's office inside the prison, Marian and Kosti had to enter the walls through two large, heavily guarded iron gates.

The warden decided to hold the concert in the prison church, but because of the large number of prisoners, Marian would have to sing two separate recitals. At the appointed time, the warden led them down several long, dark corridors to the church. An upright piano stood to one side of the altar. The first group of prisoners, whose crimes had been less serious, were waiting in their seats.

The warden told the prisoners that the great artist, Marian Anderson, had volunteered to come out and sing for them. He also reminded them that, in accordance with the custom of the prison church, there should be no applause. Marian sang for twenty minutes and ended her recital with an amusing little song called "The Cuckoo," which made the men laugh. When she finished, the prisoners applauded so strongly that it was impossible to quell them. Then one prisoner stood up and said that the men wanted to sing for Marian. They gave Kosti the music and sang a Danish song with great gusto.

The next group of prisoners was very different. "The hard, cruel, and hateful-looking faces told us that these were the worst types of criminals," recalled Kosti. "There was no kindly look of appreciation or gratitude to be found in their sinister, scowling eyes." This time the guards stood in the aisles and on the balcony with their revolvers drawn, watching every move of the prisoners.

As Marian sang, she could not tell from their hardened expressions whether the songs were affecting the men. However, the final little cuckoo song worked its charm once again, and the prisoners reacted with strong but joyless applause. "It was almost a hateful noise," observed Kosti, "though the prisoners seemed trying desperately to recover the last hidden bit of human feeling in their hardened hearts."

This hard group also sang for Marian, but their singing

had much more intensity and tension. Kosti noted that his accompaniment "was completely drowned out by these coarse sounds, which were like threatening waves in a stormy sea of contempt." Marian and Kosti left by walking down the center aisle through the prisoners and the pointed pistols of the guards. When the heavy gates of the prison closed behind them, Marian sighed and said quietly, "Lord, help their souls! Help our souls!"[26]

CHAPTER 5

Later Years

In July 1943, Marian married Orpheus "King" Fisher in a church in Connecticut. They had been friends ever since King courted Marian in Philadelphia. No matter how busy they were with their careers—Marian with her concert tours and King with his architectural career in New York—they kept in contact and somehow always knew they would get married. They were both in their early forties when they finally made that decision, but Marian said, "It was worth waiting for."

Marianna Farm

King and Marian, now Mr. and Mrs. Orpheus Fisher, bought a farm near Danbury, Connecticut, called Marianna Farm. This became Marian's second home; she would always think of the house on South Martin Street in Philadelphia where her mother, sisters, and nephew lived as her home as well.

The demands of Marian's career required that she spend most of her time on the road, but whenever she could, she went home to Connecticut for summers, holidays, and even weekends, if she was in the area. Sometimes King traveled with her, but usually his work kept him in New York or Connecticut. The time they spent together at home in Connecticut was precious to both of them. After weeks and months on tour, with endless hours spent on trains or in hotel rooms in distant cities, Marian was always glad to get back to her home and husband. Her mother and her sisters and her nephew Jimmy, who loved to visit Marian and her husband, stayed at the farm for weeks at a time. They all loved the country, but Jimmy was especially happy feeding the animals and doing farm chores.

Marian herself had always loved animals, so she was delighted to be able to look after her brood of horses, cows, pigs, chickens, dogs, and cats. In Paris, Marian had once looked after six tropical birds in the apartment she stayed in, and she had traveled all over Europe with a pet turtle by the name of Calle. However, there was no substitute for having her own animals.

In Marian's new home, she had something else she had always wanted—a place of her own in which to practice without having to worry about disturbing others. King designed and built a comfortable studio with recording equipment. It stood a short distance from the main house near a brook that ran through the property. There Marian could practice as long and as loudly as she wanted.

When Kosti returned to his native Finland to be close to his family and friends during the war, Franz Rupp became Marian's regular accompanist. Before every new season, Franz and his wife, Steffi, spent the summer on the farm so that Marian and Franz could prepare the programs for the upcoming season. Steffi, who had worked with Marian occasionally, became her official voice coach after Mr. Boghetti's death.

Every summer while Marian was "on vacation" in Connecticut, she reviewed the repertory of songs she had built up through the years and chose the ones she wanted to use in her programs for the coming season. Schubert was her favorite composer, so Marian usually went through hundreds of his songs to select the ones she wanted to sing on her next tour. Then she looked to Brahms, Schumann, Hugo Wolf, and Richard Strauss for eight to twelve more German *lieder*. Marian also chose some French songs, usually including a few by Debussy, as well as some songs in Italian and Spanish. Ever since Mr. Boghetti introduced Marian to Italian songs, she had loved singing them, but narrowing down the choice was often difficult. "There are too many things," she said, "and they are so beautiful."[1]

Marian always prepared songs in English as well, but finding songs of quality was sometimes difficult, since Marian stayed away from modern popular music. Each season she tried to sing at least one new song by an unknown American composer. She read many unsolicited manuscripts to find the right song, although she rarely found an appropriate piece that way.

It had always been her practice to conclude her programs with a group of spirituals. They were in many ways her trademark, the songs that defined her most strongly as a uniquely American artist. Her singing of these songs, which were born out of the pain and struggle of her people, always provided a powerful climax to her concerts. Marian once said about these spirituals, "They are the unburdening of the sorrows of an entire race which, finding little happiness on earth, turns to the future for its joy."

Once Marian had chosen the songs for the new season, she set about studying them and learning the intent of the composer who wrote them. With Franz at the piano, Marian recorded each song and then played it back on her tape recorder. She listened closely with her critical ear for places where she thought she could improve her performance.

Although the Fishers had help running the farm and the house, Marian gladly assumed the role of homemaker and loved the hundreds of little chores that needed to be done. She took up sewing and gardening and enjoyed improving her cooking and baking. Although she never felt completely confident in the kitchen, she collected recipes from all over the world and occasionally cooked dinner for guests.

Once when the girl who helped Marian with the housework was off and a British manager by the name of Mr. Hill was visiting, Marian decided to cook a meal for Mr. Hill, King, and herself, even though she was busy preparing for the coming season. The meal turned out to be less than a success. In fact, according to Marian, it was a disaster—the roast was burned and the vegetables and potatoes were undercooked. Everyone ended up having a good laugh over it, including Marian. Mr. Hill told Marian that he was delighted that he could now tell his grandchildren that the great Marian Anderson had cooked him a meal. Marian said she hoped he would not tell them what kind of meal it was.

When Marian and King built a modern ranch house on their property to replace the farmhouse, they had much more space and comfort. The new living room had a big fireplace and a spacious picture window that looked out over a valley, and the closets, specially designed by King, were large enough to hold Marian's many concert gowns.

Marian and King shared the task of furnishing and decorating the new house, and Marian was always thinking about what was needed at home. She spent much of her free time on the road making curtains or looking at slipcover fabrics or wallpaper samples that King had sent her. No matter how far away from home she was, in distant cities or countries, Marian was always on the lookout for items that would enhance her kitchen and home—everything from Swedish glass and Finnish plates to herbs, spices, and exotic recipes.

After years of touring the United States, Marian Anderson became so well known that there were few Americans who did not know who she was. Although the number of people who actually got to hear her concerts remained relatively small, Marian's voice was carried to millions of Americans by means of radio broadcasts and records. Polls during the 1940s showed that Marian Anderson was America's best known radio singer.

The end of the war meant that Marian could once more resume her foreign travel. In 1947, she toured Jamaica and the West Indies, where her concerts were greeted with enthusiastic applause. Marian was forced to have a throat operation in the summer of 1948, but it was successful and it allowed her to resume her career. After a tour of the United States, she returned to Europe in the spring of 1949 for the first time in ten years.

In 1953, she toured South America and then went to Japan and Korea. When Marian finished her recital at the Royal Palace in Kyoto, Emperor Hirohito presented her with a special medal. Then she flew to war-torn Korea to sing for U.S. servicemen in camps and hospitals.

When Marian returned to the United States, the city of Philadelphia honored its native daughter once again in a special way. It named in her honor a new center, built by government funds, in her South Philadelphia neighborhood. The Marian Anderson Recreation Center contained a gymnasium, auditorium, playground, and swimming pool. In this center, children of all races could learn art, music, drama, crafts, games, and sports. Marian attended the dedication, as did many of her Philadelphia friends.

Metropolitan Opera

By the 1950s, Marian had sung all over the world, but she had never sung in an opera. She was in high school when she saw her first opera, *Madame Butterfly*, performed by the Metropolitan Opera Company when it visited Philadelphia. The music thrilled Marian, and she thought it would be wonderful to sing in an opera. However, she was soon deeply involved in her concert career. Once Mary Cardwell Dawson, who had founded a black opera company, wrote to Marian about the possibility of her singing with them, but the time was not right. Then, as the years rolled by, the opportunity faded.

Stanislavsky had wanted her to sing Carmen when she was in the Soviet Union, but that had not worked out. Marian received a couple of feelers from opera houses while she was touring Europe, but she was not sufficiently interested. If she ever sang opera, she wanted to do it in her own country.

However, that was improbable, because no black had ever been invited to sing with the Metropolitan Opera.

One night in September 1954, Mr. Hurok invited Marian and her husband to attend the opening of the Old Vic production of *A Midsummer Night's Dream* at the Metropolitan Opera House. Mr. Hurok, who had brought the English company to the United States, also invited Marian and King to the party for the company afterward. Since Mr. Hurok was famous for his fabulous parties, Marian knew she would not be missed if she did not attend. She and King had an apartment in New York, so her inclination was to go back there after the opera, but she changed her mind at the last minute and went to the party to make a brief appearance. She had every intention of just saying hello and leaving.

The party was even more extravagant than Marian had imagined. Besides the members of the Old Vic company, many critics and celebrities from the music world were present. Marian and King found some people they knew. As they were talking to them, the general manager of the Metropolitan Opera, Rudolf Bing, made his way through the crowd and introduced himself to Marian. He drew her aside and asked, "Would you be interested in singing with the Metropolitan?"[2]

Marian was sure she hadn't heard him correctly because of the noise level at the party, so he repeated the question. A surprised Marian took a moment before answering. "I think I would," she said cautiously.

"Do you really think you would?" he asked.

"Yes, I would," was her answer.

Mr. Bing was immediately joined by Max Rudolf, his artistic administrator, who told Marian the role they had in mind for her was that of Ulrica, the sorceress in Verdi's *A Masked Ball* (*Un Ballo in Maschera*). Marian confessed that she was not familiar with the part. She had sung many operatic arias in her career, but she had never had any reason to learn any opera role in its entirety.

The next day, people from the Met and the Hurok office talked to see if Marian's schedule could be arranged so that she would have time for the rehearsals and for the opera itself. Then the Met sent the score of *A Masked Ball* over to the Hurok office, and they in turn sent it immediately uptown to Marian's apartment.

Marian was intrigued by the part of Ulrica. It was short, but dramatic, and it called for a vivid personality as well as a beautiful singing voice. At first, Marian thought the part might be too high for her, but she agreed to study it and audition for the Met conductor, Dimitri Mitropoulos.

On the morning of the audition, Marian was still feeling that the part might be too high. Earlier in Marian's career, the high A in Ulrica's part would have been no problem, but now Marian was much more comfortable singing in the lower contralto range. At the audition, she sang the part and reached the high A without straining, but she did not feel quite right about it. When she finished, Dimitri Mitropoulos said, "You haven't worked on it enough yet, and you don't know it thoroughly. When you know it, it will go."

Marian wasn't as sure, but she agreed to study the part some more and try again in a week or so. When she arrived at her apartment, the phone was ringing. Franz Rupp told her that Mr. Hurok was trying to reach her and that she should call him right away.

When she got Mr. Hurok on the line, the first thing he said was, "Congratulations!" When Marian asked him why, he told her that she was now a member of the Metropolitan Opera Company. "We meet at the Metropolitan this afternoon at four to sign the contract."

Marian was amazed. Another audition was not necessary, after all. Mr. Mitropoulos had called Mr. Bing right after Marian left to tell him that Marian could sing the part, and Mr. Bing had called Mr. Hurok to work out the details, all this as Marian was riding uptown. The excitement that Marian felt at hearing the news made her realize just how much she really wanted the part. She immediately called King at his office, her mother in Philadelphia, and the Rupps, who had worked so hard to help her prepare for the audition.

The next day, newspapers across the country carried the story—for the first time in history a black was to sing at the Metropolitan Opera. There could be little doubt about the significance of Marian Anderson singing at the Met. An editorial in *The New York Times* put the matter in perspective: "That Marian Anderson has fulfilled a lifelong ambition is not nearly as important as the fact that we have another opportunity to hear her in still another medium. When there has been discrimination against Marian Anderson, the suffering was not hers, but ours. It was we who were impoverished, not she."

After the contract was signed, the intense preparations began. Marian continued her voice training with Steffi Rupp and also worked with the operatic coach Paul Meyer, whom she had consulted when she was preparing for the audition. At the Met, Victor Trucco worked with Marian on the correct phrasing and tempo of the Italian libretto. Marian also worked with the stage director, Herbert Graf, on the acting aspects of her role. He made suggestions, but he always insisted, "Do the thing that seems natural to you."

Next came the sessions at the piano that integrated the singing and acting and then the rehearsals with soprano Zinka Milanov, who was to sing the principal female role, and tenor Richard Tucker. The first full dress rehearsal of the opera was in late December, at which time Marian met the chorus and orchestra. She also met the press, because the Met allowed reporters and photographers in to the rehearsal to record the historic occasion. After they finished asking questions and taking pictures, they were dismissed, and Marian and the rest of the cast got on with the dress rehearsal.

Marian enjoyed the special excitement of her work in opera—the stimulation of singing with other great voices and the camaraderie of working with a large company. It was certainly a change of pace from the solitary discipline of concert singing. Marian also liked working under the pressure of a fixed schedule. "I had to stretch my hours to crowd more activity into them, and somehow all this caused the blood to race through me with new meaning," she said. "I felt incredibly alive, able to do any amount of extra tasks. I even managed to get some of my letters answered, and that's really something."[3]

On opening night, January 7, 1955, the Metropolitan Opera House, resplendent with glittering lights, was charged with a special electricity. Backstage, Marian was excited but also reassured, knowing that out in the house her husband, her mother and sisters, and Mr. Hurok and his wife were sitting together in the center box. The lights dimmed and the orchestra played the overture. Then the curtain rose and the opera began.

When the curtain went up on Scene 2, Marian was already on stage, dressed in witch's rags and mixing a magic brew. The sight of Marian Anderson standing on that stage brought the entire audience to its feet for a prolonged standing ovation. The conductor had to stop the music until the applause died down. Marian later confessed that she was as "nervous as a kitten" and that she found the ovation unsettling: "I trembled, and when the audience applauded and applauded before I could sing a note, I felt myself tightening into a knot."[4]

When the applause subsided, Marian sang her opening aria, "Redell'a bisso." Although she said later that she was not completely satisfied with her performance because she felt she was too tense and tried too hard, everybody else loved it. One respected critic pointed out that although she wavered a little at first, she quickly reached the level of musical excellence that she had demonstrated on the concert stage, adding that the climax of the scene "was sung with such meaning that she stamped herself forever in the memory of all who listened."[5]

At the end of Act I, there was enthusiastic applause, and the audience demanded many curtain calls for the entire cast, but especially for Marian. Zinka Milanov embraced Marian on stage, and when Marian was offstage, the audience kept chanting "Anderson!" to get her to come back. The Met had a policy against solo bows, but that night Marian's fellow singers gave her a little push so that she was on the stage by herself in front of the standing, cheering audience. When Marian returned to her dressing room, she was surrounded by her family, friends, and the press. Marian's mother embraced her daughter and whispered in her ear, "We thank the Lord."

Some of the same excitement that had been present on that historic night in New York was present again the following week when the Met took *A Masked Ball* to the Academy of Music in Philadelphia. There Marian felt more relaxed, knowing that she was singing in front of so many of her friends and supporters from the church, who had contributed to her early voice studies when she most needed their help. After the performance, at the mayor's reception, Marian spoke about her dream as a little girl of one day singing with the Met at the Academy. "Tonight," she said, "the dream came true."

After her first season at the Met, Marian toured Israel with the Israel Philharmonic Orchestra. She loved the dynamism of the young nation and was moved by the spiritual echoes of its ancient and modern history. She attended a Passover seder that reminded her of her black Hebrew grandfather and the way he used to explain the Passover seder to her. She also visited the places she had sung about all her life in her beloved spirituals—the Jordan River, Jerusalem, Nazareth. She sang at a kibbutz near the Syrian border and had tea with the Israeli president and the prime minister. When she sang in Tel Aviv, she was so impressed by the young musicians she talked with that she established a scholarship fund for young Israeli singers.

On her way home, she sang in Morocco, Tunisia, Spain, and Paris, where she appeared as a soloist once again with the Israel Philharmonic, which was visiting France. Sol Hurok happened to be in Paris at the time, so he took Marian to dinner at his favorite restaurant in honor of the anniversary of their first meeting in Paris twenty years earlier. "We reminisced about our artistic partnership," Marian said, "and he toasted it with champagne."

Back home in Connecticut after the tour, Marian finished her autobiography, which she had contracted to write for Viking Press. Then, after another working summer, Marian launched into a busy year—a fall tour of the United States, more appearances at the Met, more recordings, and a spring tour of Latin America. Her autobiography, *My Lord, What a Morning*, which she dedicated to her mother, was published in October 1956.

Asian Tour and United Nations

By now Marian Anderson was one of the most admired women in the world. She was respected not only for her voice but for the courage and dignity with which she faced life. In the fall of 1957, the American government decided that Marian would be the best person to represent the United States in the underdeveloped countries of the Third World. Under the sponsorship of the State Department, she embarked on a tour of Asia that took her to twelve countries and covered over 40,000 miles. CBS sent a television crew along to record the historic trip.

Marian began her tour by returning to Korea. While she was there, Ewha Women's University in Seoul awarded her an honorary degree for her leadership in the struggle for justice and human rights. Then she visited Vietnam and Thailand. The king of Thailand paid unusual homage to Marian by rising from his throne to greet her—a sign of respect rarely given even to visiting heads of state. Marian visited many

Thai schools. She sang spirituals for the children and told them about Abraham Lincoln and the Emancipation Proclamation.

Marian then visited Singapore, Taiwan, and Hong Kong. At her next stop, in Burma, she was personally greeted by Prime Minister U Nu and his wife. They attended Marian's concert, and then went backstage to thank her for visiting their country.

Marian went next to the emerging new nation of Malaysia. She sang at a boys' school in the capital of Kuala Lumpur. Marian told the boys that the future of their young country was in their hands, and for that reason, she said, it was very important "that you not let little things like hate and fear destroy you, restrict you from being the kind of big person you could be." That night at her concert Marian became the first foreign artist ever to sing the country's new national anthem. The nation's leading newspaper hailed her gesture as "a mark of deep respect for our newborn nation."

The last part of Marian's trip took her to Ceylon, Pakistan, and India. In India she sang with the Bombay City Orchestra, the only symphony orchestra in Asia between Israel and Japan. In New Delhi, the 1,200 concert tickets offered to the public were snapped up so quickly that Prime Minister Nehru considered himself lucky to have gotten one. The Indians paid Marian their highest honor when they invited her to speak in old Delhi at the memorial to their great leader, Mahatma Gandhi, whose message of nonviolent resistance to oppression was soon to play such an important part in the civil rights struggle in America.

Marian, who made a profound impression everywhere she went, was photographed and interviewed at every turn. Because of the disturbances in Little Rock, Arkansas, where a few black students were trying to enter a previously all-white school after the Supreme Court declared segregation in the schools unconstitutional, Marian was asked about America's race troubles. The news from Little Rock was a shameful story, but Marian handled it with her usual dignity. When one reporter asked her if she would ever sing for the segregationist governor of Arkansas, Marian answered that she would if she thought it would do any good.

Asian newspapers and magazines called Marian a great singer and a great woman, and the American press praised her trip and the impact she was having on Asia. *The Saturday Review* called her tour "a cry for freedom, a national anthem, a morality lesson and a Christian hymn."[6] An American general, who had been especially worried about the effect of Soviet propaganda on the new emerging countries of the Third World, called Marian "our secret weapon," adding, "We need more Marian Andersons."

On December 30, 1957, many Americans watched "The Lady from Philadelphia" on Edward R. Murrow's popular television series, "See It Now." The program, which was about Marian's Asian tour, was described by *Newsweek* as "probably the most widely applauded show in TV history." It made an overwhelming impression on viewers and critics alike, and newspapers and magazines across the country praised Marian for what she had achieved. The *Atlanta Constitution* spoke for most Americans when it said, "Miss Anderson has done this country a great service."

The trip made a lasting impression on Marian as well. When she returned, she admitted that she had not been taught enough about the people of Asia, and that Asian cities had been little more than dots on the map to her before. "Then one went there, saw the buildings, and the seething mobs of people, sang to them, talked to people as intelligent as one finds anywhere." She anticipated the idea of the Peace Corps, which was born several years later in the Kennedy administration, when she urged more people-to-people contact. "There are great areas of the world where people need to meet Americans of equal intelligence, with common interests," she said. "Then many misconceptions will be cleared away."[7]

The impact of Marian's historic trip was extended even farther when the State Department distributed prints of the "See It Now" program to U.S. Information centers in seventy-nine countries. The program was seen in movie houses, schools, clubs, and even tents all over the world.

It was obvious that the people of Asia had responded to more than Marian's voice. They had been won over by her sensitivity and character, her desire to learn and understand, and her unique talent for bridging differences between people. President Eisenhower also recognized Marian's special ability. In June 1958, he appointed her a member of the American delegation to the United Nations for its thirteenth session.

It was a brilliant choice that paid as much honor to the United States and to the United Nations as it did to Marian, and Marian accepted. She immediately postponed her fall concert season in order to clear her calendar for her new work. She entered her U.N. office for the first time on September 19 and said simply, "I like it here."

Marian served on the Trustee Committee, which was concerned with the lands, mostly in Africa, that the United Nations supervised as their trustee. Her special responsibility was to study the Cameroons and Togoland and to report what she found back to the committee. As one of the five alternates in the American delegation, she also joined in discussions and decisions about a wide range of issues and problems.

Marian was an active, hardworking delegate whose work and personal intervention helped to speed up the granting of independence to the British and French Cameroons and Togoland. As a U.N. delegate, Marian spoke her mind when she felt she needed to. Once she had to announce that the United States opposed a special session of the U.N. General Assembly to take up the problems of the Cameroons. On that occasion she raised diplomatic eyebrows by making it clear that she personally disagreed with the official American position.[8]

Marian's integrity and hard work earned her the respect of the other members of the delegation. Henry Cabot Lodge, who was the American ambassador to the U.N. and head of the delegation, had high praise for her: "Marian Anderson was the most effective member of the U.S. Delegation. She handled all topics assigned her with great skill, and, on the personal plane, was extremely well liked and respected by all."[9] Another member of the delegation said that he knew of no other woman, with the possible exception of Eleanor Roosevelt, who had earned the respect, esteem, and affection of so many people.

The End of a Career

After her assignment at the United Nations was over, Marian resumed her singing career and continued it for six more years until her retirement in 1965. These were years full of achievement and honors, beginning in January 1959, with Marian's election to the prestigious American Academy of Arts and Sciences. Since membership in the Academy is limited to America's foremost artists, writers, musicians, and scientists, Marian's selection was a formal acknowledgment of her preeminent place in American culture.

On January 21, 1961, Marian sang "The Star-Spangled Banner" at the inauguration of the new president, John F. Kennedy, in a ceremony that was televised around the world. Marian met the president again later that same year twice in the same month—once in her capacity as one of the founders of the Freedom from Hunger Foundation, which worked with the United Nations to feed the hungry people of the world, and again when she sang in Washington to raise funds for the National Cultural Center in Washington (now called the Kennedy Center).

After President Kennedy's assassination, Marian sang in New York at a special memorial for him in front of City Hall. She sang three spirituals that moved everybody deeply because of the way they captured the pain and sorrow that most Americans felt.

President Kennedy had decided that Marian should receive the nation's highest honor—the Presidential Medal of Freedom—but he did not live long enough to present it to her personally. A little more than two weeks after the assassination, on December 6, 1963, Marian appeared before a White House audience that included members of the cabinet, the Congress, and the Supreme Court. There she received from President Lyndon Johnson the highest award an American president can give to a citizen in peacetime.

On January 10, 1964, just five weeks after she received the Presidential Medal of Freedom, Marian's mother died at the age of eighty-nine in the house in South Philadelphia that she and Marian had bought and furnished more than forty years before. Mrs. Anderson had the satisfaction of seeing her three daughters grown, settled, and living full and productive lives. Her daughter Ethel and her husband had bought the house next door, so Mrs. Anderson had the added pleasure of watching her grandson Jimmy grow up.

Marian felt great sadness at her mother's death, but she bore it with the calm acceptance her mother had done so much to instill in her. "I am only glad she lived long enough to realize her three girls appreciated the sacrifices she'd made for them and that I could do a little for her in return."[10]

Marian's long and productive career, which spanned more than four decades, came to an end with a farewell concert tour across America. Beginning on October 24, 1964, in Washington and ending six months later at Carnegie Hall in New York on Easter Sunday, Marian sang farewell concerts in cities across the country. At every concert, she was met with standing ovations by audiences who would not stop applauding until Marian had sung as many encores as they could get her to sing. To quench the insatiable need of the music public to hear Marian's voice, RCA Victor released five Marian Anderson record albums.

Marian's formal career came officially to an end in New York on April 19, 1965, when she gave her farewell concert at three o'clock in the afternoon in Carnegie Hall. Marian sang for two hours to 2,900 people, many of them friends. The audience gave her standing ovations before, during, and after the concert.

After three encores, Marian went backstage, but the thunderous applause continued. The audience simply refused to go home. Sol Hurok told Marian that the public would not let her retire. "The world will not allow it," he said. When people tried to get her to go back out on stage one more time, Marian said, "No, it is finished." But it was not finished. For half an hour, the audience kept cheering and applauding and calling her name. So Marian returned to the stage one more time for the final round of cheers and flash-bulbs. Then she went back to the dressing room, where, surrounded by reporters and friends, she said, "Now I'm going to be a homemaker."

Marian Anderson went home to Connecticut, having earned the right to a quieter, more private life, but she did not retire completely. That September, she went to Paris and sang at the World Festival of Negro Arts, which black artists from around the world attended. She also narrated Aaron Copland's "A Lincoln Portrait" on several occasions, including at the United Nations in 1976.

On Marian's seventy-fifth birthday, on February 17, 1977, she attended the benefit concert in her honor at Carnegie Hall. At the benefit, sponsored by Young Audiences, an organization that introduced young people to classical music, theater, and dance, and attended by Leontyne Price and many other well-known artists, Marian sang the Schubert "Ave Maria" and received several awards. First Lady Rosalynn Carter presented her with a special congressional medal for her "unselfish devotion to the promotion of the arts." Marian also received the Handel Medallion for her cultural contributions and the United Nations Peace Prize for her work during her tenure as a United Nations delegate.

By now Marian was no stranger to awards and honors.[11] Through the years a number of magazines and organizations had made her their "Woman of the Year," and more than thirty colleges and universities had awarded her honorary degrees. Marian was also one of the first twenty women inducted into the Women's Hall of Fame in Seneca Falls, New York.

Thousands of words have been written about what Marian Anderson has meant to her country, to her people, and to music, but perhaps the words on the citation of the Presidential Medal of Freedom, which Marian received in 1963, said it most simply and best: "Marian Anderson has ennobled her race and her country, while her voice has enthralled the world."

SOURCE NOTES

Chapter 1

1. Marian Anderson, *My Lord, What a Morning* (New York: Viking Press, 1956), p. 6.
2. Anderson, p. 18.
3. *Ibid.*
4. Anderson, p. 21.
5. Anderson, p. 38.
6. Anderson, p. 41.
7. Anderson, p. 45.

Chapter 2

1. Anderson, p. 52.
2. Anderson, pp. 53–54.
3. Anderson, p. 86.
4. Anderson, p. 69.
5. Shirlee P. Newman, *Marian Anderson: Lady from Philadelphia* (Philadelphia: Westminster Press, 1966), p. 49.
6. *New York Herald Tribune,* August 27, 1925. Complete quotation is in Kosti Vehanen, *Marian Anderson: A Portrait* (Westport, Connecticut: Greenwood Press, 1941), pp. 259–261.
7. Sol Hurok, *Impresario* (New York: Random House, 1946), p. 247.
8. Anderson, p. 91.
9. Hurok, p. 240.

Chapter 3

1. Anderson, pp. 141–142.
2. Anderson, p. 144.
3. Vehanen, p. 22.
4. Anderson, p. 144.
5. Anderson, p. 145.
6. Vehanen, p. 28.
7. Anderson, p. 149.
8. Hurok, p. 238.
9. Hurok, p. 241.
10. Anderson, pp. 156–157.
11. *New York Times*, March 10, 1935, quoted in Vehanen, pp. 265–266.
12. Anderson, p. 157.
13. Newman, pp. 89–90.
14. Anderson, p. 158.
15. Vehanen, p. 69.
16. Anderson, p. 176.
17. Vehanen, pp. 70–71.
18. Anderson, p. 177.
19. Vehanen, p. 105.
20. Anderson, p. 159.

Chapter 4

1. Anderson, p. 165.
2. *New York Times*, December 31, 1935, quoted in Vehanen, pp. 267–270.
3. Anderson, p. 168.
4. Newman, p. 96.

5. Hurok, p. 116.
6. Anderson, p. 173.
7. Vehanen, pp. 167–168.
8. Vehanen, p. 182.
9. Vehanen, pp. 185–186.
10. Vehanen, p. 196.
11. Vehanen, pp. 235–236.
12. Hurok, p. 123.
13. Vehanen, p. 238.
14. Anderson, p. 189.
15. Anderson, pp. 188–190.
16. Quoted in Janet Stevenson, *Singing to the World: Marian Anderson* (Chicago: Encyclopedia Britannica Press, 1963), pp. 176–177.
17. Anderson, p. 191.
18. Vehanen, p. 245.
19. Anderson, p. 191.
20. Vehanen, p. 246.
21. Anderson, p. 192.
22. Vehanen, p. 227.
23. Anderson, pp. 195–196.
24. Newman, p. 111.
25. Newman, p. 113.
26. Vehanen, pp. 54–56.

Chapter 5

1. Anderson, p. 198.
2. Newman, pp. 133–134.
3. Anderson, p. 301.
4. Anderson, p. 302.
5. Newman, p. 150.
6. *Saturday Review*, January 18, 1958.
7. Newman, p. 146.
8. *New York Times*, November 26, 1958.
9. Newman, p. 148.
10. Newman, p. 155.
11. For a complete list of awards and honors, see Janet L. Sims, *Marian Anderson: An Annotated Bibliography and Discography* (Westport, Connecticut: Greenwood Press, 1981).

BIBLIOGRAPHY

Books

Anderson, Marian, *My Lord, What a Morning*. New York: Viking Press, 1956.

Embree, Edwin R., *Thirteen Against the Odds*. New York: Viking Press, 1944.

Hughes, Langston, *Famous American Negroes*. New York: Dodd, Mead, 1954.

Hurok, Sol, *Impresario*. New York: Random House, 1946.

Newman, Shirlee P., *Marian Anderson: Lady from Philadelphia*. Philadelphia: Westminster Press, 1966.

Sims, Janet L., *Marian Anderson: An Annotated Bibliography and Discography*. Westport, CT.: Greenwood Press, 1981.

Stevenson, Janet, *Singing to the World: Marian Anderson*. Chicago: Encyclopedia Britannica Press, 1963.

Vehanen, Kosti, *Marian Anderson: A Portrait*. Westport, CT.: Greenwood Press, 1941.

Magazines

Anderson, Marian, "My Life in a White World," as told to Emily Kimbrough, *Ladies' Home Journal*, September 1960.

Klaw, Barbara, "Interview with Marian Anderson," *American Heritage*, February 1977.

Schonberg, Harold, "The Other Voice of Marian Anderson," *The New York Times Magazine*, December 30, 1942.

INDEX

ABOUT THE AUTHOR

Charles Patterson grew up in New Britain, Connecticut. After he graduated from Amherst College and Columbia University (Ph.D.), he taught history and literature at various schools. Now a writer and editor in New York City, he is a member of the Authors Guild, PEN, and the National Writers Union. His previous books are *Anti-Semitism: The Road to the Holocaust and Beyond* and *Thomas Jefferson*, a book for younger readers also published by Franklin Watts.